Powerful Thinking

Engaging readers, building knowledge, and nudging learning in elementary classrooms

Adrienne Gear

Pembroke Publishers Limited

Dedication

To every teacher and student searching for ways to embrace learning,
champion knowledge, and value thinking about the world around them.

Library and Archives Canada Cataloguing in Publication

Title: Powerful thinking : engaging readers, building knowledge, and nudging learning
in elementary classrooms / Adrienne Gear.

Names: Gear, Adrienne, author.

Description: Includes bibliographical references and index.

Identifiers: Canadiana (print) 20230581765 | Canadiana (ebook) 20230581846 | ISBN
9781551383637 (softcover) | ISBN 9781551389660 (PDF)

Subjects: LCSH: Reading comprehension—Study and teaching (Elementary) | LCSH:
Content area reading. | LCSH: Learning.

Classification: LCC LB1573.7 .G43 2024 | DDC 372.47—dc23

Editor: Kat Mototsune
Cover Design: John Zehethofer
Typesetting: Jay Tee Graphics Ltd.

Printed and bound in Canada
9 8 7 6 5 4 3 2 1

Contents

Preface

Whenever I finish a book, I think to myself that it is likely my last. But without fail, the year after that book is released, ideas once again begin to swirl in my brain. And after considerable swirling, another book begins to take shape up there, and eventually takes up far too much promising real estate, resulting in all sorts of mishaps, including misplaced keys and mis-checked hotels. That is when I know I need to clear some space by writing.

To be honest, this book feels, in a way, that it might actually be my last (I won't tell my publisher that, yet!). I've been teaching, writing, and presenting my lessons, stories, and thinking to teachers across the country and globe for almost 30 years. Writing books for teachers has been one of my greatest joys. You might think that, once a book has been released into the world, your job is done and your thinking stops. Not true; mine never does. My thinking about thinking, in fact, is bigger and wider and more curious than it was when I wrote my first book on reading comprehension nearly 20 years ago. And while my steadfast belief in essential, explicit instruction in metacognition and deep understanding has not faltered, my ideas have stretched. This book feels a bit like a full-circle exploration of where I started, where I am now, and what the future might hold.

I would describe myself as a practitioner. I am not a researcher, and while I do read a lot of books, articles, and research about literacy instruction, I believe my strength comes in taking big ideas, many from research, and transforming them into practical lessons; in helping teachers simplify those big ideas to help their students access them. This book will continue that trend, focusing on ways we can help students construct meaning in all areas of their learning. In a simple way, I have taken the concept of Reading Power—helping students think when they read—and stretched it into the content areas. We think when we read, yes, but we think when we do anything. Why not help students think when they learn?

The ideas in this book are not necessarily new, but are rather a new view of established concepts, a new lens through which I am inviting you to look with me. Thinking and metacognition have always been at the forefront of my work, yet have been, to some degree, limited to my literacy practice. In this book, I explore the idea of expanding this practice into other subject areas to help nudge your students to develop content knowledge alongside and through their thinking. You could consider it a next step, but I like to think of it as an essential step, not only in supporting our students' literacy learning, but also in elevating their understanding, knowledge, language, communication, and, ultimately, their powerful thinking across the curriculum.

Powerful Thinking: Engaging Readers, Building Knowledge, and Nudging Learning in Elementary Classrooms is intended to guide you in helping your students discover knowledge, wonder, and purpose about the world around them, and to make learning meaningful and accessible for every student you have the privilege of teaching. And while you embrace this remarkable profession, which some refer to as *teaching* but I refer to as *joy*, know I am right here with you, cheering you on with enormous admiration, gratitude, and respect.

Introduction

One day several years ago, I was walking through the hallway of a school I was visiting and passed by the Art room. I noticed the lights were off, but I could see students sitting at tables and could hear the teacher's quiet voice. Curious, I peeked around the doorway and was met with a bright, screen-filling image of Vincent Van Gogh's Starry Night projected at the front of the room. The students were silent, staring at the screen, while the teacher spoke to them about the painting. At first I thought she was simply describing the painting, but I soon realized she was asking the students deep-thinking questions about it, pausing between each question to allow time for quiet thinking. This is not verbatim, but I recall her saying this:

> *Look carefully into the sky—what do you see? What connections do you make when you see a sky filled so brightly with stars?*

> *Look carefully into that little town. Have you ever visited a small town? Where were you? Who were you with? Who do you think lives in that little town? Do you think the painter lives or lived there?*

> *Who do you think might have painted this? Do you think this is a picture of a place they knew well? Or do you think this came from their imagination—a place they dreamed of knowing well?*

> *Why do you think the painter made the stars look like they're swirling? Do you think the swirling stars have a message in them? What could the message be?*

> *When you look at this painting, how does it make you feel?*

Within seconds, I was completely mesmerized, transfixed by her words and that painting. Even though I had knowledge of both it and the artist, I found myself thinking much more about it than I ever had before. As I turned and resumed walking down the hallway, I realized the strategies the teacher had been using in her Art lesson were, in fact, comprehension strategies: she was inviting her students to think about questions, connections, and inferences while they viewed art. Students at this school were well-versed in Reading Power strategies, having used them in literacy lessons since Kindergarten. But this was an Art class. How was that possible?

Watching that teacher engage students in a piece of art using what I had long been referring to as reading strategies was a pivotal moment in my learning journey and was, as it turns out, the small seed that, years later, has grown into this book. Simply put, Reading Power had, at that moment, been transformed into Thinking Power. Up until then, the strategies I had been referring to as reading comprehension strategies—connecting, visualizing, inferring, questioning, etc.—had been used for, yet limited to, helping readers construct meaning in a text during a reading lesson. Now, these same strategies were being effectively used to help students find meaning in a painting. Some of you may be thinking, *Well, isn't that obvious?* We think when we read, of course, but we think when we do everything—talk to a friend, watch a movie, walk along the beach, look up at the stars, look at a painting. But I had never considered that concept in terms of classroom practice. It was only then that I began to consider that if we can successfully help students think while they read in order to deepen their understanding of text, why could we not stretch that success into all areas of the curriculum? Not that our students don't think in Social Studies or Science, but one could argue that we have an assumption of thinking in content areas, rather than the explicit instruction in thinking that is predominant in a literacy program.

Ultimately, we want our students to be engaging in comprehension (aka thinking) in all subject areas, not just when they read in literacy blocks. Therefore, literacy skills, including comprehension practice, shouldn't be limited to an ELA (English Language Arts) block, but integrated into all classroom learning environments. Even the most content-rich ELA curriculum cannot be a substitute for strong instruction in Science and Social Studies—and such instruction can help build and reinforce literacy skills. It is critical that, as educators, we begin to incorporate all that we know about reading development into curriculum and instructional practices, rather than limiting it to literacy lessons.

So how can we best support literacy through a content-rich learning environment, as well as a reading-rich one? You are about to find out! In this book, my goal is to help educators find ways to link literacy to learning by stretching comprehension instruction and practice into all areas of the curriculum. Using what we already know about the *think while we read* model used in comprehension instruction, such as in Reading Power, this book is intended to help you find practical ways to help learners *think while they learn* across every subject. I begin at the beginning, helping you find practical ways to engage learners by creating a culture of thinking in your classroom, a learning environment grounded in thinking across subject areas. We then take a brief look back at the key concepts of Reading Power for the purpose of setting the groundwork for integrating its strategies across the curriculum. We will look at simple ways to make thinking visible in your class, with a focus on the importance of developing a common language of thinking that both you and your students will actively use to explore the impact that oral language and classroom conversations have on building and enhancing comprehension.

In the fourth chapter, we will dive into developing a literacy-rich curriculum for knowledge-building and look at ways to integrate literacy skills into your subject areas. I will share lessons and anchor books to illustrate how easy it is to use texts as tools for teaching content and for increasing knowledge and vocabulary building through information read-alouds and classroom conversations. The fifth chapter is all about "the nudge"! I will share explicit, targeted lessons to help nudge your students' thinking when they are learning across the subject areas. These simple lessons will help learners construct meaning and think more deeply about the content they are learning about.

Finally, the second half of the book outlines examples of *linking thinking* in all parts of the curriculum. I will share examples of ways to integrate thinking into different content areas and units of study, including Math, Science, Social Studies, and Art.

For some, the ideas I'm presenting in this book might not be entirely new. Many of you could be well-versed in Reading Power and are already integrating comprehension instruction effectively into your literacy practice. This book is intended to show you ways to expand that instructional practice of linking thinking into all corners of your curriculum. It's like suddenly realizing a baking method you have used for years, that you know works well when you bake upside-down cake, works equally well when you bake cookies, muffins, scones, and even Yorkshire pudding! I am excited to share ideas to help you create a classroom that teaches, nurtures, and celebrates thinking, and to share lessons and anchor books to help you link your literacy skills with content learning. So sit back and get ready to shift your beliefs and to stretch your thinking and practice about reading comprehension, knowledge building, and linking thinking across the curriculum!

Teaching Powerful Thinking

Since the COVID pandemic and the changes it caused in teaching, it feels as if the role of teacher has evolved into much more than we could have ever imagined. More and more, educators are leaving their positions because they are feeling overwhelmed, and under-supported and under-funded. I see the fatigue on their faces and hear the concern in their voices: teaching is just too much. Children's mental health is severely affecting their ability to focus, to be interested or motivated to learn, to get along with others— the list goes on. So where does this leave us? We are scrambling to cover all the content we are supposed to get through, while our students are struggling just to take it all in, let alone understand it.

But if we pause for a moment and really think about the big picture, we have to ask: what is it we want most? Ultimately, if we have to narrow it down, I think most of us would say we want a class of kids who care about themselves, each other, and the world, who are motivated and engaged in their learning, and who see themselves as successful. And while we all wish we had a magic wand to wave over our class and cast that spell, we know that it's not that simple.

But maybe it is. What if, instead of a wand, we use a book? Perhaps an information book that some, if not all, of our students are interested in? Or possibly a book we recently read that fascinated us, surprised us, taught us something new, or took our breath away? Maybe we are teaching about ecosystems or life cycles in Science and choose *Whale Fall* by Melissa Stewart, which details the extraordinary impact a whale carcass on the bottom of ocean floor has on the ocean's ecosystem. And what if we put down the pencils, close the notebooks, and simply gather together around that book with our learners and read it aloud to them? And what if we talk about the book together with them, making connections to ourselves, to other books, to the world; asking questions; and adding our own thoughts and ideas into the text? What if we become mesmerized by the extraordinary images in the book and how they help us understand the text even more? What if we marvel together at what we have just learned about whales and ecosystems? And what if, the next day, we notice one of our more reluctant, reserved students taking *Whale Fall* from the display table we set up and bringing it to their desk? And what if another student notices and joins them, and they begin an engaged conversation about the book? Two students reading, talking, and thinking together about a book that they heard you read the day before and, for at least for one of them, consists of text they likely would not have been able to read on their own.

That, my friends, is Powerful Thinking: one extraordinary picture book that captures a student's attention, invites curiosity, builds knowledge, and stretches thinking, and one teacher committed less to marks than to meaning-making. And that teacher is you.

1 Why Teach Powerful Thinking?

After being in the teaching profession for almost 30 years, the one thing I know to be true is that change is inevitable. Education today looks very different now from how it did 20, 30, 50 years ago. When I think back to when I was a student, and then to my early years of teaching, I see monumental changes in how we view the role of the teacher in a classroom. Back in the day, a teacher could be described as a "sage on the stage," standing at the front of five evenly spaced rows of desks where quiet students listened to the whole-class lesson. The teacher had the Teacher's Guide on their desk and their job was to impart the content to their students. The lesson was taken directly from a literal, knowledge-based curriculum, and was often followed by a multiple-choice Social Studies or Science unit test to determine which students understood and which didn't—before the page was turned and the next lesson taught. Students were there to listen, learn, answer literal questions, memorize facts and dates, take a test, and repeat. Retelling and regurgitating was the order of the day, and students passed or failed depending on their ability to do that. Teaching thinking, engaging learners in rich classroom conversations, and inviting them to share their thoughts and ideas were not included on any teacher's to-do list. Reggio, SEL, UBD, Inquiry-based Learning, Loose Parts, and many more child-centred approaches were not even ideas yet, let alone developed programs and pedagogies.

Jump ahead to 1993, the year the world changed. From my extremely limited knowledge and analysis of global change—if I might be so bold as to pinpoint one particular event—it happened exactly 20 years ago when the World Wide Web became available to the global public. At the time, I was in my early years of teaching and not in any way aware of this event having global impact or implications on the educational world or my role in it. In fact, the actual impact of the Web on education would not be evident for several years. But if I could put my finger on just one thing that has significantly changed how teachers have taught and students have learned in the last 20 years, I would say it comes down to the simple fact that students no longer need a teacher at the front of the room to provide them with content. One tap, swipe, or scroll, and they have more content at their fingertips in one second than we could ever have provided for them in one or two—or even a year's worth of—lessons. And because of this dramatic shift in the way knowledge is accessed, the role of teacher as the presenter of knowledge came to a crashing halt and the sage on the stage had to miraculously transform into the "guide on the side." The world changed, so we needed to change. And, thankfully, we did. In the 20 years since the World Wide Web was launched, there has been no end to the shifts in our role as educators. It can, at times, feel overwhelming. But I am waving my pom-poms and shouting support from the rooftops about anything and everything that shakes up the one-size-fits-all, stand-and-lecture, assign-and-assess, and extract-the-facts-and-give-them-back models of teaching.

Here is a list of just some of the major educational focuses that have emerged over the last decade.

Education Now

Critical and Creative Thinking: students thinking broadly and deeply, using reason, logic, resourcefulness, imagination, and innovation in all learning areas

Student Agency: voice, choice, and acceptance in how students learn

Social-Emotional Learning (SEL): development of self-awareness, self-control, and interpersonal skills

Student-Centred Classroom: students, not the teacher, placed at the centre of instruction

Reflective Habits of Mind: providing time and space for students to process and reflect on their learning

Competencies Alongside Content: interconnecting intellectual, personal, and social and emotional proficiencies used with content

Individual Needs and Interests: rather than a one-size-fits-all approach

Extending Equity: access points for deep learning and thinking for every student

Soft Skills/Hard Skills: skills like teamwork, care for others, and independent thinking, alongside traditional skills like multiplication facts, capital cities, and animal classification

Preparing Students for Successful Adult Life

At first glance, we might look at this list and nod our heads enthusiastically at the number of positive changes we have seen unfold before our educational eyes over the last 20 years. But on further reflection, we could find ourselves needing to sit down and breathe into a paper bag when we consider the magnitude of the task of translating these changes into our day-to-day teaching practice. On closer analysis, each focus listed here shares the significant educational shifts in learning goals and teacher's roles brought on by the explosion of World Wide Web. In simple terms (I like simple!), if the Internet has taken away our primary role of providing students with content, now what? What is our new role? And if content material is now so widely accessible, thanks to the Internet, not to mention the rapid pace of AI technological developments, what are the new learning goals for our students?

At the 2018 World Economic Forum, Jack Ma, former teacher and co-founder of the Amazon-equivalent Alibaba Group in China, spoke about education. He said, "If we do not change the way we teach, in 30 years, we will be in trouble." He spoke of the urgent need for teachers to move away from hard skills, or knowledge-based pedagogy, and to focus instead on developing students' unique soft skills, things that computers will never able to do. These skills include values, believing, caring for others, and independent thinking. According to Ma, robots could replace humans in 800 million jobs by 2030. Moving away from knowledge-based curriculum and teaching students soft skills, according to Ma, is the only way we can ensure our students become successful in their adult lives.

In the years since Jack Ma made those comments, the AI surge has certainly proven his theory: content is everywhere, and it's being generated by AI faster than you can blink. But truth be told, at this time, content knowledge is still a foundational component of a child's education. Students are in school (or at home, if they are being home-schooled) to learn content and build knowledge about the world around them. Does content still matter? Of course, it does! But content alone is not enough anymore. To quote Ma, "We have to teach something unique. Something computers CAN'T do."

Our goal for students can still be for them to learn and build knowledge in the content areas, but that knowledge can no longer be judged by their ability to regurgitate the content back to us. What's imperative is what our students do with that content to bridge their learning and understanding, and to help them find meaning. Our mindset, therefore, needs to shift from content being the end point to content as the starting point. And since stand-and-deliver-the-content is no longer our role, we need to be looking for new ways to help all of our students make sense of the content, find meaning and think deeply, and use language and apply strategies in pursuit, not of regurgitation of facts, but of knowledge and insight. In other words, we need to teach our students to be powerful thinkers across all areas of their learning. And that, my friends, is your new role. Luckily, that is what this book is about!

Making Thinking Stick

So how do we teach thinking? How do we integrate this more abstract concept of teaching thinking and deepening understanding into everything we teach? Why not just give students a fill-in-the-blank, literal unit test and move on? Well, if we believe Jack Ma, computers will be soon be taking over those fill-in-the-blank jobs, and young adults are going to need to demonstrate skills far more sophisticated than memorizing and regurgitating facts if they are to be successful in this rapidly changing world.

Back in the day (I know I say that a lot, but I'm now officially old!), content learning was defined as knowledge-based and primarily centred around the ability of students to access, locate, gather, and retain facts for the purpose of giving them back. Units were taught through a curriculum guide and accompanying textbooks, often at a reading level most students were unable to access, which were used to provide the content. Note-taking was taught and used as an important tool for retaining information. Unit tests, often multiple-choice or short-answer, were given to test a students' knowledge of literal facts connected to the content of the unit. My Grade 6 teacher perfectly summed it up by telling us to "extract the facts and give them back." And that's exactly what we did. We learned by memorizing and regurgitating facts on tests, and that got us through high school and university with, hopefully, a solid C+/B average. Then we became teachers and carried that belief about content learning into our classrooms: facts given, facts learned, facts given back, check-check-check, repeat.

But over my years of teaching, I have often wondered if one can learn content without actually understanding it? Looking back on my own education, my answer, with 100% certainty, is a resounding YES! I can honestly say that, as a student, I learned a lot but understood very little. I wrote facts in tiny print on recipe cards, memorized them, then spilled them out onto test papers and forgot them an hour later. It's actually a little shocking to think about—memorizing hundreds of facts and then, in a matter of minutes, having them vanish from my head. How is that possible? How is it possible to get a solid B on an exam without having understood the content, and by forgetting it as soon as you have given it back? Even more important a question to consider is this: what is the point of learning something if you don't actually understand it? A fact slides into your brain, stays for a while, then slips out again, never to be seen again. What's the point?

While there have been huge steps taken away from knowledge-based teaching over the past 20 years, memorizing and regurgitating facts in content classes such as Social Studies or Science, with little or no understanding of those facts, is still being practiced in classrooms far more than we care to realize. The truth is, unless you do something to make a fact stick while it's inside your brain, it won't. It will slip out of your brain and out into the world, never to be seen again. To make a fact stick, you need something to hold it there, something like glue. And, simply put, the glue you need is thinking. Whether we are aware of it or not, there is an endless supply of that glue stored in our brain, but in order to make use of it, you need to know it's there! You also need to know *why* you need it, *where* to find it, and *how* to use it. And while, sadly, I admit my first visit to the "thinking glue store" happened long after I had graduated with my teaching certificate, the good news is that your students can discover the thinking glue now! They just need your help discovering it and learning how to use it.

Of course, the quick way to locate the glue is simply telling our students that they need to think about the book they are reading or content they are learning about. But most of us know that thinking is a complex, abstract concept and requires more than just a "don't forget to think" comment. We need to teach students the *why*, *where*, and *how* of thinking. We need to take the abstract concept of thinking and turn it into something tangible, audible, and important. Telling children they need to think just doesn't cut it. We need to talk about thinking, model our thinking, and make thinking visible and audible in our classrooms. I often ask teachers to think about the evidence of thinking in their classrooms: "If I walked into your classroom, would I SEE thinking? Would I HEAR thinking?" Thinking needs to be broken down and explicitly modeled, taught, and practiced, not just in our literacy blocks but across the content areas as well. Students need to become intimately familiar with the language of thinking and be given numerous opportunities to apply it in every subject. If our goal for our students is to help them become powerful thinkers, then surely our role is to explicitly teach them how to think.

FREE!

Thinking Glue

Help make those facts STICK!

2   Starting With Powerful Reading

While this book is about helping students think across all areas of their learning, its roots began nearly 20 years ago with Reading Power—helping students think while they read. So before launching too far into thinking, I want to lay the groundwork for this book with a brief look at reading instruction and brief revisit of Reading Power.

Reading Proficiency

Most will agree that learning to read is the most important skill children will learn in elementary school, a skill that permeates all areas of their future learning. Our primary goal, as teachers, is to help every student develop into a reader who is both proficient in the skills and engaged in the process, who walks out of our classrooms a better reader than when they walked in.

Reading proficiency can be defined as the command of two distinct and equally important skill sets: decoding and comprehension or, as I like to refer to them, *book reading* and *brain reading*. If we dive a little deeper into those two skill sets, we can see a range of very specific foundational skills required for mastering each side of the reading proficiency table.

Try using the terms *book reading* and *brain reading* when you talk to students about reading, e.g., *Active readers can "book read" and "brain read"*! *They can read all the words in the book and think about those words in their brain!* It's also helpful to use this language before a reading lesson to let students know the skill they will be focusing on: e.g., *Today we are going to be learning something that will help us with our book reading,* or *Today, I'm going to do the book reading, so you can focus on your brain reading.*

Book Reading	Brain Reading
Decoding • Phonological Awareness • Phonics • Sounding Out • Self-correction • Automatic Recognition of Familiar Words	**Comprehension/Thinking/ Metacognition** • Making Predictions • Literal Retelling • Making Connections • Asking Questions • Visualizing • Inferring • Transformed Thinking
Fluency • Pace • Phrasing • Punctuation • Intonation	

But how best to teach that? The *how* of teaching children to become proficient, engaged readers is often called into question. The debate—commonly referred to as the *reading wars*—is generally framed as a battle between two distinct views. On one side are people who advocate for an intensive emphasis on phonics—

understanding the relationships between sounds and letters—with daily lessons that build on each other in a systematic order using decodable texts. On the other side are proponents of approaches that put a stronger emphasis on metacognition and constructing meaning using authentic texts, with some phonics instructions sporadically mixed in.

Recently, this debate has again been in full force, as structured, foundational phonics skills are leading the charge in many elementary classrooms with support from popular programs such as Heggerty, UFLI, Secret Stories, and Really Great Reading. The Science of Reading movement has been successful in raising awareness of the importance of foundational skills (e.g., phonological awareness, knowledge of letters and sounds, knowledge of phonics, decoding skills). There is little doubt that these skills are fundamental to reading success and should no longer be a point of contention. *However* (you knew that was coming!), reading success requires much more than foundational phonics skills. Phonics skills are literally meaningless unless readers can make sense of words and texts, unless they can bring something of themselves into the book. In other words, comprehension counts—it always has, and it always will. As P. David Pearson stated, as he opened a keynote presentation many years ago in Vancouver, "No matter how important code is, it is not the point of reading."

If reading proficiency means being able to read the words and understand what those words mean, surely our reading instruction needs to include instruction both in phonics and in comprehension, beginning in Kindergarten. Rather than ask a teacher to choose reading instruction that teaches phonics skills, limiting reading in class to decodable texts, or to opt for reading instruction that teaches comprehension skills through more challenging texts, why not consider decoding and comprehension as complementary skills? Not *this or that*, but *this AND that*? Students do need structured phonics skills and opportunities to practice those skills with decodable texts in their literacy blocks, but they also need (and deserve) regular opportunities to engage in a literacy-rich curriculum filled with engaging, content-rich books across all areas of their learning.

Reading Engagement

There is a big difference between a student who can read and a student who loves to read. I think most of us would agree that one of our main objectives, when it comes to teaching reading, is that our students grow to love it. When we think of an engaged reader, we might visualize a child hunched over a book, eyes glued to the text and/or images, their face changing expressions, sometimes with a laugh or an open mouth. Maybe they are reading with a partner, and they are pointing to the page and talking excitedly about what they are seeing or reading about. They are hooked, can't wait to turn the page, can't wait to find another book like it, can't wait to tell someone about it. But the reality is that this idyllic state of reading engagement does not happen for every child. Each year, we encounter children who struggle to engage in books because they are too burdened by the text in front of them. Reading leaves them feeling disheartened, frustrated, and often overwhelmed.

Structured phonics provide the essential skills that students need in order to independently decode words, to know letters, sounds, blends, patterns, heart words, root words, word endings, phonemes, diphthongs, etc. But phonics

"A phonics-first approach to reading is too narrow. From the start, we must view learning to read as a language and thinking process, not just a sound-out-words process."—Regie Routman, *The Heart-Centered Teacher*, p. 114

lessons and decodable texts alone do little to instill joy and engagement in the act of reading.

In her recent book, *The Heart-Centered Teacher* (2024), literacy expert Regie Routman wisely states:

> If we view reading, as I believe we must, as reading for understanding—including for pleasure, information enrichment, personal interests and goals—all of that can happen from the earliest stages. And, of course, decoding skills are necessary. However, there are just too many variables in teaching reading to teach all learners the same way or to simplify the teaching of reading by call it an exact science... The human element must be paramount in all we teach. (pages 115–116)

Some might argue that only when they know how to read (decode) will students experience reading joy. But reading is a holistic experience, and students also need exposure to engaging books and to engaging teachers who model their excitement in learning through books; who provide equitable access to a wide range of books, texts, and genres for students to choose from; who read aloud daily from picture books, chapter books, novels, poems, and information books; who engage their students in rich class discussions about the books they are reading; who invite questions, connections, and inferences. If students lack this exposure, then I don't believe reading engagement stands a chance.

Holistic Reading Check-In

While most school districts conduct baseline reading assessments, predominantly for Primary students at the start of the school year and again at the end, it is important for teachers to continue to have regular reading check-ins with their students throughout the year, at all grade levels. These one-on-one reading conferences are helpful for tracking students' reading progress in both code and comprehension, for targeting instruction, for regulating small-group reading instruction, and for responding to the needs of individual learners. There is no better way to identify a student's strengths and "stretches" in reading than to sit side-by-side with them and listen (and watch) as they read aloud. Remember—we are teaching students, not a curriculum! More competent readers might need only one or two check-ins per term, while "up and coming readers" (my favorite new term, adopted from Regie Routman) could need more one-on-one meetings with a teacher.

The Holistic Reading Assessment checklist on pages 26–27 can be used to track each student's reading skills. Use the Class Reading Profile on page 28 to document individual results and identify appropriate reading groups, based on need rather than level. Small-group instruction should be flexible and fluid, and help target students' reading stretches as they become apparent. I suggest these steps in conducting your check-in as a guideline of what to listen for during the reading conference:

- Choose a book or passage slightly above the child's reading level (i.e., instructional level rather than individual level).
- Listen to the child read aloud.
- During reading, monitor and pay attention to these reading skills:
  Decoding: What does the reader do when they encounter unknown words? How does the reader apply phonics strategies? Do they make an attempt, use cues or clues, appeal, or stop reading altogether?

Fluency: How does the reader sound when they read aloud? Do they read in meaningful phrases, pay attention to punctuation marks, read using a good pace, and use appropriate intonation and expression?

- After reading, assess these reading skills:

Comprehension: Can the reader provide a literal retell (Beginning–Middle–End) of the text? What comprehension strategies do they apply (e.g., make connections, ask questions, infer, etc.)?

Reading Identity: What is the reader most proud of with their reading? What do they find the most difficult about reading?

Reading Power

For those who are new to Reading Power, this section provides the background into the *what, why,* and *how* of comprehension instruction (aka "brain reading") and outlines how to launch Reading Power in your classroom.

My very first book, *Reading Power*, published in 2006, is grounded in the research of P. David Pearson, who identified specific strategies used by proficient readers to help them interact with and make sense of text. My book was written as a how-to book on comprehension instruction and focused on five specific comprehension strategies, or reading powers, to help readers think while they read: connect, question, visualize, infer, and transform. The book provides practical lessons and anchor books to help teachers teach thinking—a concept that, up to that time, was not on many teachers' weekly schedule, including mine! Teachers who began using this approach noticed a significant increase in their students' comprehension skills and reading engagement as they began asking questions, making connections, drawing inferences, and gaining meaning from the books they were reading.

When I think back on how I learned to read, I can still recall my Grade 1 teacher holding up flash cards one by one, saying each word on the card, then having students repeat the word back. Over and over and over until we had memorized the words. Those same words would appear in our "Dick and Jane" readers and we would miraculously "read" them. I never actually learned how to decode, but I perfected the art of repetition and memorization. As I got older, reading in school consisted of "read this and answer the questions." Being a good reader meant finding all the right answers directly in the text, then answering in complete sentences, with a capital and a period and "don't forget the date." Like many students, I soon discovered that I didn't have to read the text in its entirety to get the answers correct. I could start with the question, skim the text to find the answer, and get 10 out of 10 comprehension questions correct, without actually having read the text. And thinking, you ask? Thinking was not part of the process. In fact, I have no memory of any of my teachers talking about thinking, teaching comprehension strategies, modeling their thinking while they read aloud, or engaging us in conversations about the meaning of a text after they read.

When it came to content subjects (Science and Social Studies), I continued the art of memorizing and regurgitating. In high school and university, I copied facts from the textbooks onto small cards and stayed up all night memorizing, only to spew it all out onto the test page the following day, not caring that an hour after the test, none of the content remained in my head. Poof! Gone!

When I became a teacher, I replicated the assign-and-assess comprehension-question routine with my own students, excited to now have a Teacher's Guide to use to mark their answers with a ✓ or an ✗. It was not until years later that I realized I was part of the *doing-comprehension* movement, rather than teaching it. And there is a big difference between *doing* reading and *teaching* reading.

I remember one day, early in my career, an ELL student was reading a passage out loud at what seemed to be a proficient level of fluency. But when I asked him a question about the text after he had finished, he replied, "I don't know." I asked him a different question; same reply. Surprised, I asked him "But aren't you thinking about the story when you read it?" After a lengthy pause, he turned to me and asked, "What does thinking look like?" Then it was me who could not respond. I made up something, no doubt, but that question haunted me. How could someone read words and not understand what those words mean? More importantly, what *does* thinking look like? That question planted a seed in me that, years later, grew into Reading Power.

At that time, my school in Vancouver had participated in a district-wide reading assessment, exposing that our school had significantly lower comprehension scores than decoding and fluency scores. Many were shocked at these results, and wondered how students were able to read fluently without understanding what they were reading. Looking back, it seems clear that it was due to the simple fact that primary teachers devote a large number of instructional hours focusing on teaching students how to decode, but the same was not being done to teach students how to think! The test scores resulted in our staff implementing a new three-year school goal: improving comprehension across the grades. The only problem was that nobody really knew what that would look like, and so a committee was formed. Turns out I was the only one who volunteered to be on the Comprehension Committee. I *was* the committee!

Coinciding with my becoming the comprehension committee, I was working on my Master's degree at the University of British Columbia and, in one of my reading research classes, was introduced to the work of P. David Pearson—in particular, to his extensive research into comprehension instruction. With his research—along with the work of Stephanie Harvey, Anne Goudvis, Ellin Keene, Debbie Miller, and Richard Allington—as my foundation, I developed an approach I believed would help teachers who, like me, were "doing" comprehension rather than teaching it. I called the approach Reading Power. Reading Power is grounded in metacognition and provides readers with five specific reading strategies they can use to help them construct meaning when they read: connect, visualize, question, infer, and transform (synthesize). I did not make up these strategies; they are grounded in research. What I did was transform a concept from research into something practical for the teachers at my school to use so that buy-in would be high.

With most of the staff on board, we launched into our first year of Reading Power. I made Reading Power posters for every classroom. Because of my passion for using picture books to anchor my literacy lessons, I began gathering and creating Reading Power Book Bins for the teachers to use. We had a lot of meetings and made a lot of mistakes but, overall, worked tirelessly to get the program up and running.

Our end-of-year reading assessments, while not as significant a miracle as I had hoped, showed enough improvement in comprehension scores to conclude that something was working. The staff agreed to continue using the approach the following year, adding more nonfiction into our Reading Power lessons. I started giving workshops, then I wrote a book—and the rest, you could say, is history.

Reading Power has continued to evolve and, in the nearly 20 years since its inception, my thinking about thinking has grown and stretched. What has become more and more clear to me is that, while the original goal of Reading Power might have been to help improve reading comprehension, what has resulted is ultimately more important—reading engagement. When readers are able to put themselves into the texts they are reading, to add their own voice, thoughts, connections, and questions, they are ultimately more interested. As Toni Morrison so beautifully states: "The words on the page are only half the story. The rest is what you bring to the party."

The Isolate vs Integrate Debate

When I developed Reading Power almost 20 years ago, P. David Pearson's groundbreaking concept of teaching comprehension strategies, as opposed to assigning comprehension questions, was just beginning to emerge in classrooms. Teachers everywhere were beginning to teach their students to make connections or make inferences when they were reading. Since then, some have questioned whether teaching comprehension strategies in isolation is, in fact, helping students develop into strong readers. Many have criticized Reading Power, due, in part, to the fact that it teaches comprehension strategies, or powers, in isolation.

I agree that if you teach the strategies in isolation and then stop teaching altogether, students will be less likely to develop strong comprehension. Your students will likely be able to make a connection or ask a question in isolation when you tell them to, but they are not likely to apply or integrate the strategies independently. If our end goal is to have our students integrate comprehension strategies naturally and efficiently, I am firm in the belief that they first need the *why* (strategies are important) and the *how* (to use them), and need to have a language to articulate their thinking. Isolation before integration.

My best analogy for the isolate vs integrate debate is that of teaching a child how to swim. Swimming instructors would never dream of bringing their non-swimmers down to the deep end of the pool in the first lesson and expect the children to be able to dive in and swim across to the other side. Learning to swim is broken down into very small, isolated steps: becoming comfortable in the water, putting your face in, learning to blow bubbles, learning to float, learning to kick, and so on. Each skill is named, modeled, and practiced in isolation before moving onto the next. Only when a child has learned them all would they be expected to put all those skills together, dive in to the deep end, and swim. Similarly, why would teachers open a book and expect their students to dive in and apply a range of comprehension strategies to engage in the text and construct meaning, if students have never been introduced to them, don't know why or when to use them, and don't understand how they fit into the big picture of reading? Ultimately, the purpose of teaching comprehension skills is to help our students succeed in their pursuit of engagement, knowledge, and deep understanding of what they read. This is no easy task, and getting there takes time and effort. We need to start slowly, introducing and practicing comprehension strategies one at a time, before we can expect students to dive in. But what is crucial is the understanding that, while the process of teaching comprehension strategies in isolation is important, it's not the end. It's only the beginning.

Launching Reading Power in Your Classroom

Teaching students to think while they read is laying the foundation for developing powerful thinkers, for students thinking in all areas of the curriculum. Integrating thinking into all areas of your teaching needs to start small: integrating thinking into your reading program. For those who are not familiar with Reading Power, the outline here highlights the important steps in launching Reading Power in your classroom and provides the *why* and *how* of thinking when you read to your students. Once students learn how to add thinking, construct meaning, and ultimately become more engaged in books they are reading, they will more easily and effectively be able to apply those skills to their learning in other subjects.

SET CLASS READING GOALS

In a literacy lesson early in the school year, clearly explain to students that learning to read involves two different skill sets:

- *Book* Reading: being able to read the words in the book
- *Brain* Reading: being able to understand what those words mean

Work together to develop an anchor chart of Class Reading Goals. Reinforce these goals in whole-class or small-group reading instruction by clearly identifying which skill set you will be focusing on:

Today, I am going to be teaching you something that will help you with your book reading (or brain reading)!

Class Reading Goals	
Book Reading We can…	**Brain Reading** We can…
☐ Decode words using • letters and sounds • chunks and blends • patterns ☐ Read fluently using • pace • punctuation • intonation • phrasing	☐ Understand the words by • paying attention to our thinking • making connections • visualizing • asking questions • inferring what the author is trying to tell us • transforming our thinking

MAKE THINKING VISIBLE

Use a visual poster to help students understand what thinking looks like. Use the poster often to reinforce the concept and language of thinking, particularly when teaching a Reading Power lesson. (I often hear teachers admit that their Reading Power poster is hanging in their classroom, but they rarely refer to it!)

Some teachers invite students to create their own personalized Reading Power visual. See page 39 for a reproducible template. This template is also included in *Reading Power*, 2nd edition.

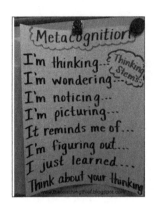

USE AND PRACTICE THE LANGUAGE OF THINKING

Create and post an anchor chart with thinking prompts in your classroom (see example in margin). Use the language as often as you can when sharing your thinking. Try to integrate the language into both literacy and content lessons. Encourage students to use the thinking language when they are talking about their thinking. Praise them when you hear them using it!

USE THE GRADUAL RELEASE MODEL

1. **Introduce** (1 lesson): Name and explain the strategy you are going to be focusing on; e.g., Connecting.
2. **Model** (at least 2 lessons): Read aloud a story to the class and model the strategy, pausing in the middle of the story and telling the students what you are thinking about:

   This part of the story reminds me of...

   Use sticky notes or a visual thought bubble when you are modeling. Use the language of thinking as often as possible when sharing: "I'm visualizing...," "I'm inferring...," "I'm connecting..."
3. **Guided Practice** (2 lessons): Invite students to participate in a group lesson. Pass out one sticky note or thought bubble on a craft stick to each student. Read a story aloud and invite students to pay attention to their thinking. Students can hold up their hand or their thinking bubble, or use a hand signal when they want to share their thinking; e.g., make a connection, ask a question, etc.
4. **Independent Practice** (2 lessons): Students can choose a book from the Reading Power Book Collection (see below) and read it either independently or with a partner. They can use sticky notes to mark their thinking or record their thinking on a response sheet.

READING POWER BOOK COLLECTIONS

Use picture books that help support a specific Reading Power strategy to help your students experience greater success. Read aloud *daily*! Tell students you are doing the "book reading" so they can focus on their "brain reading." Suggested themes for each strategy:

- **Connect:** family, friendship, feelings, school, pets, family activities, etc.
- **Visualize:** rich descriptions, sensory language, seasons, weather, locations (e.g., the beach, a mud puddle, the snowy park), etc.
- **Question:** fairy tales, fantasy, books with engaging covers and titles, books about such issues as poverty, bullying, war, etc.
- **Infer:** wordless picture books, books with little text, books where the author leaves things out for readers to fill in, etc.
- **Transform:** books that help students find new ways to think about a concept: courage, friendship, community, love, compassion, kindness, patience, etc.

Sexsmith Elementary School library, Vancouver, BC.

For more information about Reading Power and Reading Power book collections, see my book *Reading Power* (Pembroke, 2006; 2nd edition, 2016).

ORAL LANGUAGE

Provide daily opportunities for students to turn-and-talk about their thinking with a partner, or in small or whole-class groups, after a read-aloud. Encourage them to use the language of thinking (using prompts if necessary): "I'm wondering about…," "I'm making a connection to…," etc.

Use the 1, 2, 3 TALK! technique—Think for 1, Talk for 2, Share for 3—to encourage all students to engage in conversations about their thinking:

Think for 1 minute by yourself (except it's usually less!)
Talk for 2 minutes with a partner
Share for 3 minutes with the class

Reading Power Strategy Top Tips

When teaching Reading Power, there are several key concepts for each strategy that might help students be more successful. The Top Tips on pages 29–33 outline these concepts in student-friendly language and could be helpful in guiding your explicit instruction.

Notes on Top Tips

- I developed BIBB, or Bring It Back to the Book, as a strategy to help students move away from random or quick connections and bring their thinking back to the text. For more on this lesson, see *Reading Power* 2nd edition, pages 51–52.
- The concept of Brain Pockets is not based on scientific research (I just made it up!) but has been used effectively in *Reading Power* (pages 45–47) as a way of helping students understand that thoughts stored in different places in our brains can help us find connections when we read, and in *Writing Power* (pages 32–34) to illustrate the different ideas writers can use for different types of writing: e.g., *Your memory pocket is a good resource for personal narrative writing; your fact pocket is a good resource for nonfiction writing; and your imagination pocket is a good place to source ideas for story writing.* See the lesson on page 71 of this book for a more detailed introduction to Brain Pockets.

Holistic Reading Assessment

Name: _____ Grade: _____ Date: _____

Title: _____ Current Reading Level: _____

Decoding / Phonics Knowledge	Consistent evidence	Working on it	Requires attention	NA	NOTES
ATTEMPT Does the reader attempt to decode unknown words? Or do they guess, skip, stop, or appeal for help?					
INITIAL SOUNDS Does the reader know/say the initial sound when sounding out a word?					
CHUNKING Does the reader attempt to split the word into chunks or phonemes? Find little words within the word?					
SOUNDING Does the reader say each sound within the word and then blend them together?					
CLUES Does the reader use visual or other clues when reading (e.g., look at the pictures)?					
KNOW Does the reader demonstrate automatic recognition of some familiar words (e.g., *the, and, is, but, can*, etc.) ?					
SELF-CORRECTING Does the reader attempt to self-correct if they have made an error or skipped a word? Are they aware when they make a mistake or do they simply continue reading?					
Fluency	Consistent evidence	Working on it	Requires attention	NA	NOTES
PACE Does the reader read at a smooth, steady pace? Not too slow or too fast?					
PHRASE Does the reader use proper phrasing? Are they reading groups of words for meaning rather than word for word (i.e., "robot reading")?					
PUNCTUATION Does the reader pay attention to punctuation marks? Pause at periods? Use voice to indicate questions or exclamations?					
INTONATION Does the reader's voice rise and fall effectively?					

Pembroke Publishers ©2024 *Powerful Thinking* by Adrienne Gear ISBN 9781551383637

Comprehension: Literal	Circle the Appropriate Level			Prompts
RETELL Is the reader able to retell the gist of the story: i.e., outline the main events in their own words without excessive additional details?	Accurate retell beginning/ middle/ end	Parts missing or too many details	No attempt or very limited	*Can you tell me, in your own words, what this story is about?*

Comprehension: Interactive	Circle the Appropriate Level			Prompts
CONNECTION Is the reader able to make a connection to the story?	Deep-thinking	Quick	Unable	*Can you tell me about one connection you made to this story?*
QUESTION Is the reader able to ask a question related to the story or text?	Deep-thinking	Quick	Unable	*What are you wondering about this story/text/character?*
VISUALIZE Is the reader able to describe a visual image from the story?	Deep-thinking	Quick	Unable	*If you close your eyes and think about this story, what picture do you visualize (see in your mind)?*
INFERENCE Is the reader able to add a relevant idea to the story that was not written directly in the story?	Deep-thinking	Quick	Unable	*What feeling do you get when you read this story? What part made you feel that way?*
TRANSFORM Is the reader able to extend their thinking beyond the literal story and articulate message, theme, etc.?	Deep-thinking	Quick	Unable	*Why do you think the author wrote this story? What did this story make you think about?*

Reader's Identity

What are you most proud of about your reading? _____

_____

What is something about reading that is hard for you? _____

_____

Assessment Analysis

Based on this assessment, this student needs support with:

DECODING: _____

FLUENCY: _____

COMPREHENSION: _____

READING IDENTITY: _____

Pembroke Publishers ©2024 *Powerful Thinking* by Adrienne Gear ISBN 9781551383637

Holistic Reading Assessment: Class Summary Sheet

Date: _____   Grade: _____

Student	Level	Decoding	Fluency	Comprehension	Needs-Based Reading Groups
1.					1.
2.					
3.					
4.					
5					2.
6.					
7.					
8.					
9.					3.
10.					
11.					
12.					
13.					4.
14.					
15.					
16.					
17.					5.
18.					
19.					
20.					

Pembroke Publishers ©2024 *Powerful Thinking* by Adrienne Gear ISBN 9781551383637

Top Tips for Making Connections

A connection is when something in the book reminds you of something you have experienced or already know.

Remember...

- Not all connections help you understand the story better!

- Be sure your connections are connected to the heart of the story. BIBB it, Baby! **Bring It** (your thinking) **Back to the Book.**

- Just say NO to Quick Connections that are random and not connected to the heart of the story. Focus on Deep-Thinking Connections: connections to feelings, experiences, and characters in the story, or the main topic of information books.

- Use your Brain Pockets to help you find connections! Your Memory Pocket, Fact Pocket, and Imagination Pocket are filled with thoughts that will help you understand what you are reading.

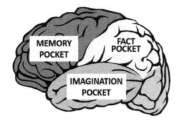

→ **Memory Pocket** for when you are reading stories and information about real-life experiences

→ **Fact Pocket** for when you are reading nonfiction and true information texts

→ **Imagination Pocket** for when you are reading imaginary stories

Pembroke Publishers ©2024 *Powerful Thinking* by Adrienne Gear ISBN 9781551383637

Top Tips for Visualizing

Visualizing is when the words in the book help create a mental image in your mind.

Remember...

- A visual image is not a picture you see with your eyes. It's a thinking picture you see in your brain!

- You need to Train your Brain to visualize! Practice visualizing with your eyes opened and with your eyes closed, and see which one works better for you.

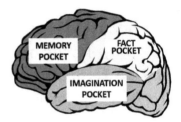

- You have hundreds of mental images in your brain! Use your Brain Pockets to help you find your visual images.

- Visualizing isn't just about what you see. Try using all your senses when you visualize: sight, sound, taste, smell, touch, and feelings.

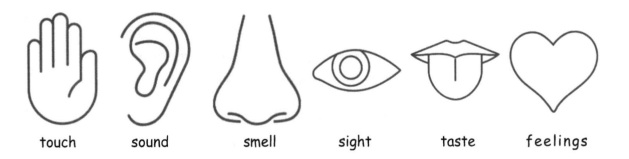

touch   sound   smell   sight   taste   feelings

Top Tips for Asking Questions

Asking questions while you read helps you clarify what's happening in the book and helps you stretch your thinking!

Remember…

• Active readers ask questions before, during, and after they read.

 • Quick Questions help clarify what's happening in the story (thinking STOPS once we know the answer).

 • Deep-Thinking Questions help stretch our thinking (thinking keeps GOING when we don't know the answer).

 • Not all questions help you understand a story better. Make sure your questions are connected to the main idea of the story. BIBB it, Baby! **Bring It** (your thinking) **Back** to the **Book.**

Pembroke Publishers ©2024 *Powerful Thinking* by Adrienne Gear ISBN 9781551383637

Top Tips for Inferring

Not all authors write everything in their books! Inferring is when you use clues the author does write and add your own thinking to help you understand what the text is about.

Remember...

- You already know how to infer. You infer every day, you just might not realize it!

- Less inking means more thinking! Good writers leave spaces for our thinking. Inferring is when a reader notices the spaces and fills in what's missing.

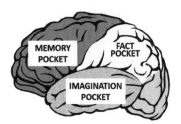

- Use your Brain Pockets to help you find your inferences. Go to where you know!
- Start your inferences with "Maybe..." or "I think..."
- Best places in a story to infer: character traits, emotions, themes.

Pembroke Publishers ©2024 *Powerful Thinking* by Adrienne Gear ISBN 9781551383637

Top Tips for Transforming

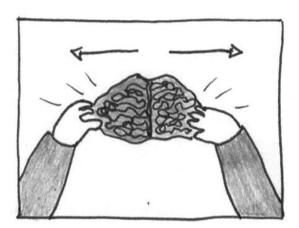

Transforming is when a thought in your head stretches or gets rearranged because of something you read.

Remember...

- A transformed thought does not erase or replace the original thought. It's the same thought, only now it looks and sounds a little different. It's like your thinking stretches!

- Books can sometimes change the way we think, feel, or act.

- Not all books are transforming. Sometimes we can read a book and enjoy it, but it hasn't changed our thinking.

- Transformed thinking often happens after you finish reading. You might reflect and notice that your thoughts are different. You might say, "I'd never really thought of it that way before."

Pembroke Publishers ©2024 *Powerful Thinking* by Adrienne Gear ISBN 9781551383637

3 Expanding to Powerful Thinking

In this chapter, I will outline ways to incorporate the power of thinking in all areas of teaching, beginning with making thinking visible in your classroom. For those already familiar with Reading Power, this will be familiar territory, but with a slight reset.

As I explained in the Introduction, the concept for this book grew from the roots of *Reading Power*. If Reading Power can help students think more deeply when they read, why limit that thinking to our literacy blocks? Why not expand that concept into our content areas—social studies, science, and the arts? Rather than having reading comprehension as our goal, why not broaden that to learning comprehension? By integrating a culture of thinking in our classrooms, we can engage our students in thinking in every subject.

Creating a Culture of Thinking in Your Classroom

The start of the school year is often a blur of responsibilities and activities as you get to know your students, establish classroom routines, conduct baseline assessments—the list goes on. Setting up a positive learning environment in our classrooms and helping our students feel a sense of belonging, comfort, and care has become one of our primary goals as we welcome new learners into our classrooms each fall. But for the purpose of this book, I am promoting an addition to that to-do list: setting up a thinking environment!

A classroom grounded in metacognitive thinking is filled with curious children building knowledge through speaking, listening, and engaging in rich classroom conversations about subjects they are excited to explore and eager to learn about. Thinking is also inclusive—students who struggle with independent reading or writing can still be active thinkers! If our goal is to develop a community of learners who think deeply across the curriculum, then thinking needs to be at the forefront of our classroom practice and integrated into everything we teach. This means beginning the school year with a clear, explicit introduction to thinking skills, and fine tuning an awareness of who we are as learners and thinkers early enough in the school year that all students become familiar and comfortable with both the concept and the language.

To align yourself and your learners with a culture of thinking, it's important to be explicit. Never assume your students are naturally metacognitive. Break it down, then build it up! Be clear from the very beginning of the school year that your class is a *thinking* classroom, and that thinking is the key to learning and understanding. Transform the abstract concept of thinking into a living, breathing, can't-live-without-it part of living and learning. Share your excitement about thinking, and your students will soon be excited too.

Here are some key questions you can introduce to and explore with your students when building a culture of thinking in your classroom:

- *What is thinking?*
- *What does thinking look like?*

- *What does thinking sound like?*
- *How does thinking help my learning?*

This first lesson is intended to be used as a starting point for introducing thinking to your students.

Lesson: Let's Talk About Thinking

This lesson, adapted from one in *Reading Power*, takes the abstract concept of thinking and transforms it into a tangible, visual framework. I have taught this lesson in many classrooms and at many different grade levels to introduce the concept of metacognitive thinking and to answer the question: *What does thinking look like?* It also helps to introduce to your students the language of thinking that will be key in developing strong communication skills in your class.

For those of you already using Reading Power in your literacy lessons, think of this as a simple reset: extend the concept, visual, and language of thinking you use with reading into all areas of your teaching. Explain clearly to your students how thinking when you read can be stretched to "thinking when you learn."

- Write the word *Thinking* on the chart stand or whiteboard. Tell students you want to spend a few minutes talking about thinking today, but before you begin, you want them to spend a minute thinking about thinking. Invite them to take a thinking pose as they think about their thinking!
- After a few seconds, ask students if any of them found it difficult to think about thinking. Why? (*Don't know what it looks like, hard to describe*) Tell them that you sometimes find it hard to think about thinking, too.
- Write the word *apple* on the board or chart stand. Say the word and tell students that you want them to think about an apple. Allow a few seconds for them to think. Ask students to compare when you asked them to think about thinking with when you asked them to think about an apple. Which was easier? (*Apple was easier because we know what it looks like and we have personal experiences with an apple.*)
- Pass out paper. Invite students to draw a picture of an apple on their paper. Allow only about 30 seconds for them to draw. Invite students to share and compare their apple picture with a partner.
- After partner sharing, ask students to look at their apple picture and put their hands up if their apple

  - has a roundish shape
  - has a stem
  - has a leaf
  - has a shiny spot or any shading
  - has a worm
  - has a bruise, etc.

- Ask students if they felt that drawing an apple was easy or hard (*Most will say easy*). Ask why (*Because we know what it looks like, we have tasted it, held it, etc.*).
- Tell students to turn their papers over and draw a picture of thinking. Many students will draw thought bubbles—let them!
- Draw a thought bubble on the chart stand or whiteboard. Say

  I'm noticing many of you are drawing thought bubbles. Now, thought bubbles are not wrong. We see them in comics and cartoons and graphic novels. But thought bubbles are more of a symbol for thinking. We all know that thinking doesn't actually happen in a bubble above our heads. So if you did draw a thought bubble,

I'd like you to redo your picture to try to show what thinking looks like inside *your head when it's actually happening.*

- Allow more time for drawing. Invite students to share and compare their thinking picture with a partner.
- Invite some students to share and explain their thinking pictures with the class. Tell students you are noticing how different everyone's thinking pictures are. Ask students which was more challenging: drawing a picture of an apple or drawing a picture of thinking (*Most will say thinking*). Ask why (*Because we don't really know what thinking looks like*).
- Explain to students:

> *One of my goals for you this year is that you will all become deep thinkers. We know thinking is important* all the time—*when we read, when we learn, when we look at a pictures, when we watch a movie, when we talk to our friends. But because we can't really see it, sometimes we forget about it; we don't focus on it or pay attention to it. It's harder because we don't really know what thinking looks like. Maybe if I could look inside someone's head, I might be able to see what thinking looks like.*

- Bring out the Thinking Power poster on page 39 or simply draw an outline of a head and shoulders on the whiteboard. Tell students you are very excited to be able to show them exactly what thinking looks like!
- One at a time, place the pieces of thinking inside the brain: *Connect, Question, Visualize, Infer, Transform.* Say each word and explain that these thinking powers can help us understand things better.

> *It's like putting a little bit of our own thinking into the book we are reading, or adding to the information we are learning about in Math or Science or Social Studies. Asking questions, making connections, visualizing, inferring, and transforming can help us think and understand things a little better. Some of you might use these thinking powers when you read to help you understand the story better. But this year, we are going to use these thinking powers all the time: when we read, when we do math, when we do social studies and science and art, and even when we watch a video! We are all going to become deep thinkers and deep learners, because our busy brains are going to be actively thinking all the time!*

- Pass out the Thinking Power template on page 39 and invite students to create a personalized visual of themselves as thinkers.

  Early primary teachers can sing this "Thinking Power" song (adapted from *Reading Power*) with your students to the tune of Frére Jacques:

  We all have a BUSY BRAIN,
  busy brain, busy brain!
  We all have a busy brain.
  Five cheers—THINKING POWER!
  Hip hip, Connect!
  Hip, hip, Question!
  Hip, hip, Visualize!
  Hip, hip, Infer!
  Hip, hip, Transform!
  Hooray for THINKING!

Primary teachers may choose to demonstrate looking for thinking inside a student's head. Invite a student to stand up beside you. Make a pretend telescope with your hands and "look" into the student's head. "No, I definitely can't see Jacob's thinking!"

Thinking Power poster on page 39 is adapted from the Reading Power poster in *Reading Power*, 2nd edition (2016).

For a more detailed description of each of these strategies, see page 30 of *Reading Power*, 2nd edition.

A visual image of a thinking brain can really help students, both in primary and intermediate grades, to grasp the concept of what thinking looks like, as well as reinforcing the language of thinking. Those of you who use a Reading Power poster or visual can simply replace the word *Reading* with *Thinking*.

Tools for Teaching Thinking

Thinking Anchor Books

When creating a culture of thinking in your class, it never hurts to have a few anchor books on hand to reinforce and promote the concept of deep thinking to your students. Share these books about thinking or great thinkers throughout the year and reflect on how the book—or character in the book—illustrates thinking.

The Boy and the Sea by Camille Andros

On A Beam of Light: A Story of Albert Einstein by Jennifer Berne

The Crayon Man: The True Story of the Invention of Crayola Crayons by Natascha Biebow

Your Fantastic, Elastic Brain by JoAnn Deak

The Boy Who Loved Math by Deborah Heiligman

The Girl Who Thought in Pictures by Julia Finley Mosca

Sarabella's Thinking Cap by Judy Schachner

The Boring Book by Shinsuke Yoshitake

Thinking Prompts

TALK ABOUT YOUR THINKING!
This makes me think about…
This makes me realize…
This reminds me of…
I'm wondering…
I'm visualizing…
I'm inferring…
I'm feeling…
I'm surprised/shocked that…
I used to think… but now I'm thinking….

In my experience, most elementary students have not yet developed a language to talk about their thinking. When asked to share their thinking about a book, for example, we might get, "I liked it. It was good," or "I didn't like it. It was boring." If we want our students to be skilled thinkers, we must give them the linguistic tools of the trade! I recommend posting a Talk About Your Thinking anchor chart, with a list of thinking prompts (see sample in margin) that your students can refer to when talking about their thinking. Posting an anchor chart will be not only a helpful reminder to your students, but also a reminder to you!

Modeling Your Thinking

One of the most effective ways we can encourage our students to engage in thinking is to model our own thinking at every opportunity. As with Reading Power, once the concept, thinking visual, and language have been introduced, we need to continue to reinforce them by showing our students what thinking looks like and sounds like in real time. It's important to be intentional about integrating thinking skills into all aspects of our teaching, embedding it into Social Studies, Science, Art, Music, and Math. The more our learners see and hear us talking about our thinking in all subjects, the more likely they are to start activating their own.

In my book *Reading Power*, I introduce the concept of *read-aloud–think-aloud*. This is when, during a class read-aloud, you pause and tell your students that you need to just stop reading for a moment because you want to share your thinking. Many primary teachers hold up thought bubbles when they are sharing their thinking about a book. Some use sticky notes or thinking bookmarks to mark a page where they made a connection or asked a question. Some of you might be quite comfortable modeling your thinking during a read-aloud, but now I'm encouraging you to stretch that modeling into your subject areas. Depending on your comfort level and grade, I recommend using a simple cardboard thought bubble attached to a ruler or pointer, which you can hold up to model your thinking. During a Math, Science, or Social Studies lesson, pause, hold up a thought bubble (or not), and share your thinking. For example during a Science lesson on simple machines, you could model this way:

Now, learners, I just need to stop for a moment here and share my thinking. When I was sharing this information about a shovel being a lever, I was actually making a surprise connection! I do a lot of gardening, but it had never occurred to me that my gardening shovel was actually a lever, and that holding the shovel on an angle when I am digging makes it easier to lift than if I tried to lift it straight up. Is anyone else making a similar connection?

Thinking Power

Name: _____   Date: _____

Fill your brain with Thinking Power

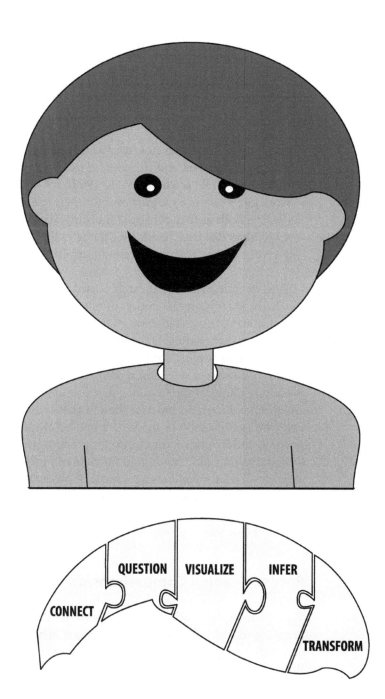

4 Doing a Teaching Reset

At the end of the 20th century, extensive research into reading comprehension was being conducted. In particular, P David Pearson's research, among many other studies at the time, looked carefully into what good readers do, specifically asking them to think aloud during their reading process. From these studies, researchers determined reading to be a complex, active process of constructing meaning. The act of constructing meaning is

- **Interactive:** It involves not just the text being read but also the reader interacting with the text and the context in which reading takes place. (Heilman, A. W., Blair, T. R., & Rupley, W. R. 1998)
- **Strategic:** Readers have purposes for their reading and use a variety of strategies and skills as they construct meaning. (Baker, L., & Brown, A.L., 1984)
- **Adaptable:** Readers change the strategies they use as they read different kinds of text or as they read for different purposes. (Dole et al., 1991)

This was the primary research I used when developing my Reading Power approach, specifically the notion of interacting with text and the idea that comprehension is constructed through the merging of the reader with the text before, during, and after reading. Since *Reading Power* was first released in 2006, research and practice in reading comprehension has continued to evolve. And while this book is not focused solely on reading or reading instruction, its roots lie in my work in reading comprehension. As a proud practitioner, I know that my books are grounded more in practice than in theory and research; however, as someone who is constantly in the reflect-and-refine state, I believe that educational research and its impact on classroom practice needs to be central to the evolution of teaching and learning. In the field of medicine, for example, wouldn't we all prefer a doctor conducting a medical procedure that is groundbreaking and based on relevant research to someone still using a procedure practiced 30 years ago? Why should it be different in the education field? What changes should be considered or made to keep research at the forefront of our practice?

Recent Reading Comprehension Research

Since Pearson's groundbreaking work in the 1990s, important new research has been added to his findings, shedding new light on the complexities of reading comprehension. Many of you will be familiar with the Scarborough Reading Rope diagram, created by H.S. Scarborough in 2002, depicting two necessary intertwining braids or ropes that contribute to the act of reading. The diagram represents the two essential components outlined in the Simple View of Reading, a research-supported formula of the reading process that views reading as having

You can read more about the Active View of Reading in Jennifer Kelly's book *Active Reading Classrooms* (2023).

two basic components: word recognition (decoding) and language comprehension (understanding) (Gough & Tunmer, 1986). In 2021, Nell Duke and Kelly Cartwright proposed an adaptation of this model they call the Active View of Reading. Instead of describing reading comprehension as the product of two components, decoding and language comprehension, they introduced two new cognitive skills that research shows play an important role in reading comprehension: self-regulation and the bridging process.

While I am not going to spend too much time unpacking these models of reading, I would like to explore three specific findings from current reading research that have a direct impact on how we might develop comprehension, stretch thinking, and nudge learning: constrained and unconstrained reading skills, language comprehension, and knowledge building.

Constrained and Unconstrained Reading Skills

In their book *This Is Balanced Literacy Grades K–6* (2019, pp. 6–7), authors Fisher, Frey, and Akhavan use the terms *constrained* and *unconstrained* to refer to the skill development of both code and comprehension skills in early childhood literacy programs. The terms were originated in an article by Dr. Scott Paris in 2005 and are still being used by researchers to understand the effects of early childhood literacy programs and interventions (Bailey, Duncan, Cunha, Foorman, & Yeager, 2020). These terms highlight the main differences between the code of reading and the meaning of the text. Code-based skills are *constrained*, which means they are mastery-based: once we learn them, we know them. Comprehension skills are *unconstrained*, which means we continue (throughout our life, not just when we hit level 30!) to learn and grow into them, based on the situation and context, and on the ever-evolving experiences and knowledge that readers bring to text.

Code (words)...	Comprehension (meaning)...
• represents *constrained skills* • is mastery-based: once we learn it, we know it • includes alphabet, letters, sounds, etc. • acts as a bridge to take readers toward meaning • often uses precise assessments to determine if a child "can read"	• represents unconstrained skills • is conceptionally unbounded: learning continues, even into adulthood • includes vocabulary, background knowledge, cognitive skills, etc. • relies on skills that are ongoing, continually evolving • often uses less-precise assessments

As adults, when we tackle a new, unfamiliar text as proficient readers, we stretch our ability to interact and make meaning of the text, especially if the topic and vocabulary are not found within the confines of our background knowledge (in other words, if your "fact pocket" is empty!). Mastery of constrained skills, according to Fisher, Frey, and Akhavan, should not be viewed as the end of reading instruction. Ongoing development of unconstrained skills (language, knowledge, and thinking) is imperative and should be viewed as an obligation by all teachers. In this current period of prominence of code-based skills, it's an important reminder that reading is a process, and that what a reader brings to the text is as important as their ability to decode it.

Language Comprehension

Language comprehension, one of the two strands in Scarborough's model, is the ability to derive meaning from spoken words; reading comprehension is the ability to derive meaning from print. In his book *Reading Instruction: Two Keys* (2006), Dr. Matthew Davis, Director of Reading at the Core Knowledge Foundation writes,

> Even the best phonics-based skills program will not transform a child into a strong reader if the child has limited knowledge of the language, impoverished vocabulary, and little knowledge of key subjects. (p. 15)

To understand this a little better, let's look at an example. Let's say a student in your class has general difficulty with reading comprehension because they are struggling with decoding skills. That student could, in fact, comprehend a text about sharks or reefs because their parents are marine biologists and because they have accumulated a significant ocean-related language—made up of words, phrases, and facts—from their parents. Yet this same student might not comprehend a text about environmental sustainability because they lack the language and knowledge of the topic. Successful reading comprehension, according to Davis, often depends on the language of a text, because the greater a reader's funds of background knowledge about a topic, the stronger their comprehension. Alternatively, students from disadvantaged backgrounds might struggle with reading comprehension, despite being able to decode accurately and read fluently. They are often believed to have poor reading comprehension ability when, in fact, it is their lack of language comprehension (overall knowledge and vocabulary) which is the root cause. Davis believes that language comprehension is a key aspect of reading comprehension that is currently being overlooked in many classrooms.

Knowledge Building

I was first introduced to the concept of *knowledge building* through a series of articles by the Scientific Advisory Committee's Knowledge Matters Campaign that focus on how educators can support literacy by bringing knowledge building into their classrooms to strengthen comprehension and get children excited about learning:

> While foundational language skills and the Science of Reading approach is beyond dispute and should no longer be a source of discord... building knowledge of the natural and social world is also essential to developing strong readers who can not only decode words but also comprehend what they are reading... Building knowledge need not—and should not—wait until students possess some level of foundational reading skills. (ASCD 2023)

We know all too well the importance of background knowledge and the impact it has on comprehension. Anyone who has ever scratched their heads while trying to read a car manual without knowing the first thing about the context or vocabulary in front of them can attest to the fact that background knowledge plays a significant role in one's ability to comprehend. Reading research over the last 40 years has increasingly emphasized the importance of background knowledge as a major contributor to the reading ability of students (Smith, R., Snow, P., Serry, T., & Hammond, L., 2021; Duke, N. & Pearson, D., 2002). While other factors could be at play, readers with more general knowledge about the world tend to have an easier time understanding new information.

As educators, we are fully aware that many students who walk into our classrooms at the start of a new school year lack substantial background knowledge that will help them develop strong comprehension skills. I often hear teachers comment that it's challenging to teach a strategy, such as making connections, because of how little background knowledge many of their students have. In my years of working with teachers, background knowledge is often referred to with negative undertone, as a *Have* or *Have not* label, sometimes with a little blame and judgment mixed in. Some might even consider background knowledge as a child's responsibility—they either have it or they don't.

But why should any child be held accountable for the background knowledge they bring into a classroom? Background knowledge begins developing long before a child enters school and is primarily dependent on their daily interactions at home with caregivers. Families who engage their children in conversations, games, outdoor play, outings, and language-rich activities; families who share knowledge and talk to their children about the world around them—such families play a significant role in early development of background knowledge and a child's *schema*. (If you are familiar with my concept of Brain Pockets, you would say these children's brain pockets are full!) Often, these families are privileged, educated, and from higher-economic backgrounds. But where does that leave the others, the children who suffer from inequitable opportunities to gain background knowledge before they enter school?

As the equity movement in education continues as an important and prominent theme, we understand that it's our responsibility to help level the playing field and support all students on their path to becoming readers, writers, thinkers, and learners. In other words, background knowledge, or lack thereof, is not a child's responsibility. Rather than blaming or complaining that students lack background knowledge, we need to help every student build knowledge in our classrooms. It is therefore our responsibility to create a rich learning environment that can helps every student build knowledge, to be better able to understand and retain new information they are encountering. And "knowledge" is not simply acquiring new facts. Knowledge building is helping students develop thinking they can apply to new information so that the content is meaningful and sustainable.

See *Funds of Knowledge: Theorizing Practices in Households, Communities and Classrooms* (Gonzalez, N., Moll, L.C., & Amanti, C., 2005).

Background Knowledge	Building Knowledge
• Knowledge a child **brings** with them into the class (from home) • Funds of Knowledge	• Knowledge a child **builds** in class • Knowledge that is not made up of literal facts, but of facts *plus* thinking

Family/Caregivers

Teachers

In a recent *Forbes* article I read, author Natalie Wexler, author of *The Knowledge Gap*, discusses a meta-analysis of more than 50 studies of comprehension strategy instruction that highlight some of my key points. The findings show that comprehension strategy instruction in isolation is not helping students develop into strong readers. The study found that many teachers who teach isolated reading strategies often do so with texts that students have limited or no background knowledge with, in other words, students lack the language comprehension to support their reading comprehension. Unless that knowledge (or vocabulary) is provided before reading, regardless of the strategy being taught or practiced, meaning is often missed. Diving a little deeper, the study reveals that a quick injection of background knowledge to help students understand an isolated text they are about to read does little to build their understanding over time. For students to gain the kind of knowledge that will help them understand the text, they need longer periods of time with same-subject texts; for example, using a collection of texts connected to subjects you are teaching in Social Studies or Science when teaching comprehension strategies. Linking comprehension instruction to topics you are already teaching, and using a collection of books on that topic, helps students build knowledge and vocabulary connected to that subject, and can lead to stronger comprehension.

Reflecting on the Research

So what does this new research and these new concepts (constrained and unconstrained reading skills, language comprehension, and knowledge building) tell us about reading comprehension and overall literacy development? What clearly stands out to me is that comprehension strategy instruction alone will likely not result in better, stronger readers. There are other factors at play, namely our students' language comprehension and background knowledge, that strongly influence their ability to understand what they are reading. Teaching comprehension strategies cannot make up for a student's lack of knowledge. If our goal is to help our students become powerful readers and thinkers, we need to refine our instruction, taking into account their language comprehension and the funds of knowledge (Gonzalez, N., Moll, L.C., & Amanti, C., 2005) they bring to their reading and their learning, recognizing that not all students bring equal funds of knowledge into our class. We also need to reconsider the value we are placing on constrained reading skills and remind ourselves that reading instruction does not end when a student has mastered the code. Unconstrained reading skills are life-long and deserve equal instructional time in a holistic reading program.

Putting Research into Action

So now what? Research findings are one thing, but classroom practice is a whole different ball game! (Lucky for you, this is my favorite part. Batter up!) What does all this research look like in my classroom? I have heard many stories recently of teachers who are feeling overwhelmed with the huge responsibilities they now face in their reading programs with the strong focus on foundational "book reading" skills. Trying to fit in all the phonics lessons is hard enough, so it's understandable that time for comprehension and "brain reading" might be limited.

Reading Power lessons have been, up to now, primarily taught during literacy blocks, most often using fiction anchor books. But what if we consider comprehension as not being limited to reading instruction, but as extended across all areas of learning? Rather than feeling overwhelmed that your literacy blocks are overflowing, why not consider linking thinking across the curriculum? In other words, why not consider developing a literacy-rich curriculum, in which reading, writing, listening, and speaking are woven into every subject every day by bringing content-rich texts into our content lessons? What if we used texts as tools and merged brain-reading practice into every subject we teach?

"How would I do this?" you might be asking. How do we embed thinking into everything we teach? The answer might be easier than you think. If you are an early primary teacher, your book-reading instruction (aka phonics) can still be at the forefront of your literacy blocks. But brain-reading instruction (aka comprehension) can be integrated into all of your subject areas.

Let's explore practical ways to help learners build knowledge, develop vocabulary, and extend thinking across the curriculum through the following:

- **Literacy-Rich Curriculum:** integrate literacy practices into your content classes (Science and Social Studies)
- **Content-Rich Texts:** increase information/nonfiction content-rich texts in your classrooms
- **Content-Rich Text Sets:** build nonfiction text sets connected to your content subjects
- **Content-Rich Interactive Read-Alouds:** give content-rich read-alouds a central role in your classroom
- **Literacy-Rich Conversations:** facilitate and engage students in interactive conversations during read-alouds

A Literacy-Rich Curriculum

A literacy-rich curriculum encourages frequent reading, writing, listening, and speaking, regardless of the content areas. While not a new idea, "literacy-rich curriculum" is certainly a recent buzzword in literacy! By developing literacy-rich curricula, we not only help students build knowledge, interest, and understanding in the subjects they are learning, but also naturally provide opportunities for them to strengthen their comprehension through reading, writing, listening, and speaking in all subjects. Powerful thinking can only really be successful in a literacy-rich classroom, where students are engaged and excited about the subjects they are learning about.

While researching for this book, I came across an interesting article on "The Dinosaur Effect" that, for me, clearly illustrates what is at the heart of a literacy-rich, content-rich classroom. Have you ever had a student that was a walking encyclopedia of information on a particular subject? Often, very young students can rattle off the names of every warplane in the First and Second World War, or every dinosaur that ever walked the planet, or the name, number, and points average of every hockey player who ever passed a puck in the history of the Boston Bruins (true story!). This is what the article refers to as "the dinosaur effect," the capacity for young children to capitalize on their passionate interests and retain astounding stores of knowledge. Not only that, but large, multi-syllabic vocabularies connected to their favorite topics seem to stick (there's the thinking glue!) the instant they are exposed to them.

"All aspects of a skill grow and develop as subject-matter familiarity grows. So we kill several birds with one stone when we teach skills by teaching stuff. Moreover, there is evidence that by teaching solid content in reading classes and teaching reading in content classes, we increase students' reading comprehension more effectively than by any other method."
— Hirsch (2003, p. 28)

To read this article in it's entirety, go to https://knowledgemattterscampaign.org/post/scaling-the-dinosaur-effect/

With their huge bank of background knowledge, these children are motivated to use their emerging decoding skills and immerse themselves in high level texts about their passion. But put that same child in a guided reading group and give them an isolated decodable or leveled text on a random topic for which interest and background knowledge is non-existent, the child demonstrates anything but proficiency in reading.

So, what does the dinosaur effect tell us, and how does it connect to a literacy-rich content-area classroom? As educators, we can take advantage of this natural learning motivation in two ways:

- **Enhancing Student Engagement:** When children are engaged in topics they are interested in, they are far more motivated to want to read, write, speak, and engage in learning.
- **Exposure to Text Sets:** Multiple related content-rich text sets students read (or have read to them) deepen their engagement, interest, knowledge, vocabulary, and comprehension.

Many of you reading this, particularly early primary teachers, are likely already immersed in structured, foundational reading instruction, also known as Science of Reading or SoR. Widely recognized structured SoR curricula—for example, UFLI, Heggerty, Jolly Phonics, and Secret Stories—are being implemented in early primary classrooms across the United States and Canada at a staggering rate. Incorporated into many of these programs are decodable books: simple books written for beginning readers that contain the specific grapheme–phoneme correspondences students have recently learned. Decodables provide readers an opportunity to use their segmenting and blending skills to help develop the ability to recognize words quickly and effortlessly, rather than having to guess or predict them from pictures or context clues.

Some of you reading this might rightfully believe that sequential decodables need to be used *before* children can move on to more advanced texts. For the record, I have never doubted that foundational skills, including phonemic awareness, knowledge of sound–letter relationships, decoding and spelling skills, and fluency, are essential. But as I stated earlier, I stand firmly in my belief that foundational skills alone are not sufficient for readers to become fully literate. Master decoders who can read all the words, but who lack interest, knowledge, vocabulary, and ultimately the meaning of the text, are not proficient readers. Yes, instruction in decoding skills is paramount in a child's reading success, but so, too, is comprehension instruction. Yes, decodable texts play an important role in practicing sequential sounds, but so, too, do content and language-rich literature to engage in, interact with, and ultimately be inspired by. (It's hard to think deeply about "The cat on the mat has a hat.") What's important to remember is that, when we teach students to become readers, it is imperative that we expose them to a range of different types of texts, not just decodables. If beginning readers have only narrow opportunities to read different kinds of texts, they have very narrow opportunities to learn and build knowledge as they get older (Cabell & Hwang, 2020; Cervetti & Hiebert, 2018).

I recently read a comment on a SoR group chat on Facebook by a teacher who had made the decision to remove all the books from her classroom that her Grade 2 students couldn't independently decode. Picture books, information books, comic books, joke books, poetry books, how-to books—all boxed and hidden away. It was decodables or nothing. "Having books in my classroom that my students can't read is harmful and has a negative impact on their progress and self-esteem," she explained. I almost cried, thinking about the students in that classroom not having access to real books. There are so many other positive reasons for children to be holding a book in their hands than to successfully decode the words! Engaging, content-rich information books, in particular, hook kids in with fascinating facts and real-life photos about the wonders of the world around them. One does not need to be able to decode every word on the page to be drawn into a book about humpback whales, the planet Jupiter, or baby elephants; to look and learn and wonder and talk about what is on the pages. Yes, phonics instruction is important; yes, decodables are excellent tools for practicing new sounds. But real kids deserve real books. A literacy-rich curriculum emerges from real books about real topics students are interested in and are learning about.

So instead of a strict, steady diet of instructional-level decodable texts, students need a wide range of engaging texts in every subject. A literacy-rich classroom is filled with content-rich books that provide learners with a window into the world, and we, their teachers, provide a bridge to that window. Whatever unit of study is being taught includes a collection of content-rich texts connected to the topic. The books are shared throughout the unit for regular interactive read-alouds (more on the read-alouds on page 54) that engage students in listening, speaking, and thinking. After reading the book aloud, it can be added to a special Topic Table, where content books are displayed. (We have all experienced the phenomenon of a book, after it is shared with our students, becoming the hot pick for independent reading.) Yes, students need phonics instruction and decodable texts, but they also need to be immersed in literacy-rich classrooms where interesting, engaging information books connected to subjects they are learning about and are interested in are regularly within their hands, their ears, their heads, and their hearts.

TIPS FOR BUILDING A LITERACY-RICH CURRICULUM

See pages 50–54 for book recommendations.

- Gather text sets of content-rich books connected to your units of study (Social Studies, Science, Math, etc.).
- Use these books often for interactive read-alouds during content or literacy lessons.
- Invite students to "Think for 1, Talk for 2, Share for 3" (see page 24) before, during, or after the read-alouds.
- Use the texts as tools, and model, model, model a variety of thinking strategies before, during, and after reading (see lessons on pages 58–84).
- Have a Knowledge Building Table in your classroom for displaying text sets connected to a unit of study.

Content-Rich Texts

Anyone who knows me knows how much I love books. Not just a little. I'm talking heart-stopping, book-sniffing, would-have-a-sleep-over-in-a-book-store-if-I-could book joy. I have always believed that authentic children's literature is the single most important teaching tool in every elementary classroom—from K to Grade 7. Picture books have always been my teaching partners. In fact, I can't recall a time I started a lesson, whether literacy or content, without a picture book in my hand. Whether it be a lesson on making connections in reading, using sensory details in writing, or learning about food chains in science, picture books help me anchor my lessons, engage my students, and bring book joy into my classroom. And it's not just me. More and more teachers I work with comment on how often they use children's literature in their literacy lessons. One might conclude that, to some degree, literacy practices in elementary schools might be viewed as more engaging than content subjects, because literacy teachers tend to create print-rich environments and incorporate engaging activities, such as daily read-alouds and active class discussions. Subject areas like Social Studies and Science, on the other hand, tend to focus more on knowledge or facts about a particular topic or unit of study, and are often accompanied by textbooks, but might lack the engaging print-rich environment of literacy lessons.

Many years ago, I came across a quote in Stephanie Harvey's book *Nonfiction Matters* that shocked me:

> Over 80% of the classroom books fell into the fiction category. Considering about 80% of the reading we do outside of school is nonfiction, it wasn't hard to recognize a disconnect. (Harvey, 1998)

But after considering this for a time, I realized she was accurately describing the majority of classroom libraries I had encountered, including mine! Nonfiction texts are not often our go-to picks for conducting engaging read-aloud lessons with our students. More often, we associate our literacy lessons with fictional narrative. Certainly, when it comes to Reading Power strategies, most of my anchor book recommendations are categorized as fiction. When I survey teachers at my workshops, most will admit that the majority of their read-alouds and classroom libraries are heavily weighted toward fictional text. Yet, much research shows that most young readers enjoy nonfiction and may even prefer it to fiction (Clark & Teravainen-Goff, 2020; Correia, 2011; Ives et al., 2020).

The world of content-rich nonfiction books available for young readers has undergone extensive and dramatic changes over the past decade. Many of today's information books look nothing like nonfiction did when I was young. Alphabetized library shelves filled with encyclopedias, my only source of information when I was a child, have been replaced by an abundance of exceptional informational picture books on every subject you could ever want to learn about. Finely crafted nonfiction children's books have the power to inform, inspire, and get kids fired up about learning. They feature stunning visuals, rich language, and dynamic designs that capture curious minds and invite young readers to think about topics in new and exciting ways. Quite simply, these content-rich books play a huge role in engaging kids, stretching their thinking, and nudging their learning. And research supports this by clearly showing that nonfiction can enhance a child's literacy development and fuel their natural sense of wonder about the world and how it works (Hwang, H., Lupo, S. M., Cabell, S. Q., & Wang, S., 2021; Duke, N. K., Ward, A. E., & Pearson, P. D., 2021).

One of the simplest, yet most important, things we can do to develop thinking, increase knowledge, and build language comprehension in our classrooms is to increase our collections of nonfiction books.

"Unlike many textbooks and materials written for online or print-based school curriculum, nonfiction literature for young people does more than communicate information. Nonfiction literature contextualizes primary source evidence, offers multiple perspectives on current and historic events, and shares new scientific discoveries." — NCTE Position Statement on the Role of Nonfiction Literature (K–12) (2023)

Why not choose a nonfiction author for your next Author Study? Explore the author's background, interests, and books, and discover how nonfiction authors research and share their facts!

Here is a list of popular nonfiction series and engaging authors I would recommend for any classroom or school library.

NONFICTION SERIES	NONFICTION AUTHORS
Fly Guy Presents series by Tedd Arnold	Jason Chin
I'm Trying to Love series by Bethany Barton	Nicola Davies
Disgusting Creatures series by Elise Gravel	Candace Fleming
Over and Under series by Kate Messner	Douglas Florian (nonfiction poet)
Two Truths and a Lie by Ammi-Joan Pacquette	Gail Gibbons
Who Would Win? series by Jerry Pallota	Elise Gravel
Truth or Lie (Step into Reading) by Eric S. Pearl	Steve Jenkins
A First Book of… series by Scot Ritchie	Kate Messner
Let's Read and Find Out series by various authors	Kadir Nelson
Little People, Big Dreams series by various authors	April Pulley Sayre
Rookie Readers series by various authors	Joyce Sidman (nonfiction poet)
Scholastic Canadian Biography series by various authors	Seymore Simon
Scholastic True or False series by various authors	Melissa Stewart
National Geographic Readers	Jeanette Winter
Time for Kids books	
Magic Treehouse Fact Tracker	

Content-Rich Text Sets

"Libraries are not just nice to have; they are crucial for ensuring equitable opportunities and joy for all students." — Regie Routman, *The Heart-Centered Classroom*, page 155

Sarah Murdoch Black, teacher-librarian at Quigley Elementary School in Kelowna, recently updated her nonfiction section with large, clear dividers she purchased from Merchandising Libraries Australia. In the short time since she added them to the library shelves, she has seen a remarkable increase in nonfiction book sign-outs!

Teachers often comment that one of their challenges when teaching content subjects is finding enough content-based books at independent-reading levels for their students to read or use for research. And while I agree that independent reading of nonfiction texts is important, content knowledge, along with print knowledge, language comprehension, and oral language, can be simultaneously developed when students participate in content-rich read-alouds. The goal here is simple: if you want to help support powerful thinking in your classroom, build content-rich text sets! If you are fortunate enough to have a qualified teacher-librarian in your school, connect with them about upcoming topics or units of study and ask for their help in gathering content-rich text sets. Invite them into your classroom to do mini book talks about some of the titles to get students engaged and excited.

During either your literacy or content lessons, use these books as read-alouds, exposing your students to content through engaging information and vocabulary, and provide opportunities for them to think and talk about their learning. Having a text set, as opposed to a single title, is important here—be sure to have multiple related nonfiction books connected to your unit of study. When I say "set," I don't mean 20 books! I would consider five books on the same subject a set. Don't worry too much about reading level, as these are books you will be using for your interactive read-alouds (see pages 50–54), and then adding to a Knowledge Building Table or display in your class for your students to revisit. In my experience, the more students learn about a topic, the more they want to learn! When texts connect with and extend students' content knowledge, students will likely want to read more books on their own. Remember, you don't have to read nonfiction books in their entirety. Even a single page can be used for

See page 118 for lessons and book list on Community.

See pages 111–112 for lessons and book list on Social Justice.

CONTENT-RICH TEXT SETS

your read-aloud. Be keen about content! Show your excitement about what you are learning from the books, alongside your students. Knowledge can be highly motivating, and seeing you excited about a subject will excite and inspire your students!

Here are my recommendations for getting started on building your own content-rich text sets. You will find some fiction books included in these lists, which have been added because they are based on true events, include factual back matter, or connect to the topic in a supportive way.

SOCIAL STUDIES

Activism
Rise Up and Write It by Nandini Ahuja
I Can Do It Too! by Karen Baicker
Follow the Moon Home: A Tale of One Idea, Twenty Kids, and a Hundred Sea Turtles by Philippe Cousteau
If You're Going to March! by Martha Freeman
Something, Someday by Amanda Gorman
The Pink Hat by Andrew Joyner
No Voice Too Small by Lindsay H. Metcalf
Speak Up! by Miranda Paul
One Too Many by Linda Grace Smith

Ancient Civilizations
The Gods and Goddesses of Olympus by Aliki
Mummies Made in Egypt by Aliki
Escape from Pompeii by Christina Balit
I Am the Mummy Heb-Nefert by Eve Bunting
National Geographic Kids Everything Ancient Egypt: Dig Into a Treasure Trove of Facts, Photos, and Fun by Boyer Crispin
Mummies, Pyramids, and Pharaohs by Gail Gibbons
How We Lived in Ancient Times: Meet Everyday Children Throughout History by Ben Hubbard
The McElderry Book of Greek Myths by Eric A. Kimmel
See Inside the Ancient World by Rob Lloyd Jones
See Inside Ancient China by Rob Lloyd Jones
See Inside Ancient Egypt by Rob Lloyd Jones
You Wouldn't Want to Be a Roman Gladiator! Gory Things You'd Rather Not Know by John Malam
Cleopatra by Diane Stanley

Disinformation/Fake News
Can You Believe It? How to Spot Fake News and Find the Facts by Joyce Grant
Killer Underwear Invasion! How to Spot Fake News, Disinformation & Conspiracy Theories by Elise Gravel
Fake News: A Funny Illustrated Book of Facts for Kids! by Clive Gifford
True or False: A CIA Analyst's Guide to Spotting Fake News by Cindy L. Otis

Early Humans
Inch and Grub: A Story About Cavemen by Alastair Chisholm
Ug: Boy Genius Of The Stone Age And His Search For Soft Trousers by Raymond Briggs
When We Became Humans: Our Incredible Evolutionary Journey by Michael Bright
Afterward, Everything was Different: A Tale From the Pleistocene by Jairo Buitrago
The First Drawing by Mordicai Gerstein
My Best Book of Early People by Margaret Hynes
Stone Age Boy by Satoshi Kitamura
You Wouldn't Want to Be a Mammoth Hunter! by John Malam

Evolution
It Started with a Big Bang: The Origin of Earth, You and Everything Else by Floor Bal
The Story of Life: A First Book about Evolution by Katherine Barr
When We Became Humans: Our Incredible Evolutionary Journey by Michael Bright
Life on Earth: The Story of Evolution by Steve Jenkins
Our Family Tree: An Evolution Story by Lisa Westberg Peters
On the Origin of Species by Sabrina Radeva
Out of the Blue: How Animals Evolved from Prehistoric Seas by Elizabeth Shreeve
Charles Darwin's Around the World Adventures by Jennifer Thermes
Grandmother Fish: A Child's First Book of Evolution by Jonathan Tweet

Life Through Time: The 700-Million-Year Story of Life on Earth by John Woodward

Explorers
Far Beyond the Garden Gate: Alexandra David-Neel's Journey to Lhasa by Don Brown
The Great Voyages of Zheng He by Demi
Dare the Wind: The Record-breaking Voyage of Eleanor Prentiss and the Flying Cloud by Tracey Fern
Shackleton by William Grill
Great Adventurers: Incredible Expeditions of 20 Explorers by Alastair Humphreys
The Top of the World: Climbing Mount Everest by Steve Jenkins
Keep On! The Story of Matthew Henson, Co-Discoverer of the North Pole by Kathleen Krull
Life in the Ocean: The Story of Oceanographer Sylvia Earle by Claire A. Nivola
Explorers (100 Facts) by Dan North

Kids Book of Canadian Exploration by Anne Maureen Owens
Canadian Explorers by Maxine Trottier

First Contact/Fur Trade
Louis Riel Day: The Fur Trade Project by Deborah L. Delaronde
Encounter by Brittany Lundy
Encounter by Jane Yolen

Government
The Kids Book of Canadian Prime Ministers by Pat Hancock (first pages)
The Art of the Possible: An Everyday Guide to Politics by Edward Keenan
Canadian Government by Elizabeth MacLeod
How to Build Your Own Country by Valerie Ryan
The Governing Canada series by Elizabeth Simon
Who Runs This Country, Anyway?: A Guide to Canadian Government by Joanne Stanbridge

---

SCIENCE

Animals and Animal Adaptation
Animals in Winter by Henrietta Bancroft
Animal BFFs: Even Animals Have Best Friends! by Sophie Corrigan
Find Out About Animal Camouflage by Martin Jenkins
Actual Size by Steve Jenkins
Biggest, Strongest, Fastest by Steve Jenkins
Creature Features by Steve Jenkins
What Do You Do When Someone Wants to Eat You? by Steve Jenkins
Hiders Seekers Finders Keepers: How Animals Adapt in Winter by Jessica Kulekjian
Lifetime: The Amazing Numbers in Animal Lives by Lola M. Schaefer
Peculiar Primates: Fun Facts about These Curious Creatures by Debra Kempf Shumaker
Pipsqueaks, Slowpokes, and Stinkers: Celebrating Animal Underdogs by Melissa Stewart
Summertime Sleepers: Animals That Estivate by Melissa Stewart
Tree Hole Homes: Daytime Dens and Nighttime Nooks by Melissa Stewart

Biomes/Ecosystems
Walk This Wild World: Lift the Flap by Sam Brewster

The Boreal Forest: A Year in the World's Largest Land Biome by L.E. Carmichael
Many Biomes, One Earth by Sneed B. Collard III
At the Poles by David Elliot
The Tide Pool Waits by Candace Fleming
Bringing Back the Wolves: How a Predator Restored an Ecosystem by Jude Isabella
The Night Flower by Lara Hawthorne
Shady Streams, Slippery Salamanders by Jason Patrick Love
Creekfinding: A True Story by Jacqueline Briggs Martin
Who's Hiding on the River? by Katharine McEwen
Who's Hiding in the Woods? by Katherine McEwen
Around Antarctica: Exploring the Frozen South by Tania Medvedeva
Nature's Patchwork Quilt: Understanding Habitats by Mary Miche
Over and Under series by Kate Messner (includes *Desert, Canyon, Rainforest, Oceans, Ponds*)
Welcome to the Neighborhood by Shawn Sheehy
Creep, Leap, Crunch! A Food Chain Story by Jody Jensen Shaffer
A Strange Place to Call Home: The World's Most Dangerous Habitats & the Animals That Call them Home by Marilyn Singer

Whale Fall: Exploring an Ocean-Floor Ecosystem by Melissa Stewart

Earth Day/Earth Conservation
Taking Care of Our Mother Earth by Celestine Aleck
If You Come to Earth by Sophie Blackall
What Does it Mean to Be Green? by Rana diOrio
The Great Big Green Book by Mary Hoffman
Old Enough to Save the Planet by Loll Kirby
The Earth Book for Kids: An Introduction to Earth Science by Dan R. Lynch
My Friend Earth by Patricia MacLachlan
Be a Good Ancestor by Leona Prince
Thank You, Earth by April Pulley Sayre
My First Book of Earth: All About Our Planet for Kids by Stephanie Manka Schuttler
10 Things I Can Do to Help My World by Melanie Walsh
Let's Take Care of the Earth by Rozanne Lanczak Williams

Electricity
Charged Up: The Story of Electricity by Jacqui Bailey
Timeless Thomas: How Thomas Edison Changed Our Lives by Gene Barretta
Switch On, Switch Off by Melvin Berger
Electricity for Kids by BooksGeek
The Magic School Bus and the Electric Field Trip by Joanna Cole
Oscar and the Bird: A Book about Electricity by Geoff Waring

Force and Motion
Isaac Newton (Pocket Bios) by Al Berenger
Go Bikes, Go! by Addie Boswell
Forces Make Things Move by Kimberly Bradley
Forces: Physical Science for Kids by Andi Diehn
Motion at the Amusement Park by Tammy Enz
I Like to Move It! by Professor Beaver
The Gravity Tree: The True Story of a Tree That Inspired the World by Anna Crowley Redding
Motion! Push and Pull, Fast and Slow by Darlene Stille
Explore Forces and Motion! With 25 Great Projects by Jennifer Swanson
Zombies and Force and Motion (Monster Science) by Mark Weakland

Human Body
The Universe in You by Jason Chin
The Body Book by Nosy Crow
Tiny Creatures: The World of Microbes by Nicola Davies
Power Up: Your Incredible, Spectacular, Supercharged Body by Seth Fishman
X-Ray Me!: Look Inside Your Body by Felicitas Horstschafer
Bones: Skeletons and How They Work by Steve Jenkins
Kay's Anatomy: A Complete (and Completely Disgusting) Guide to the Human Body by Adam Kay
Weird But True Human Body: 300 Outrageous Facts about Your Awesome Anatomy National Geographic Kids
Gross and Ghastly: Human Body by Kev Payne
Your Amazing Digestion from Mouth through Intestine by Joanne Settel (poetry)
Look Inside Your Body by Louie Stowell
Human Anatomy for Kids: A Junior Scientist's Guide to How We Move, Breathe, and Grow by Kristie Wagner

Insects
A World of Bugs & Insects: A Kid's Guide to the World's Most Fascinating Insects by Tim Babler
I'm Trying to Love Spiders! by Bethany Barton
Heads and Tails Insects by John Canty
Insects & Bugs for Kids: An Introduction to Entomology by Jaret C. Daniels
The Backyard Bug Book for Kids by Lauren Davidson
Not a Buzz to Be Found: Insects in Winter by Linda Glaser
The Fly by Elise Gravel
Jumper: A Day in the Life of a Backyard Jumping Spider by Jessica Lanan
Insect or Spider?: How Do You Know? by Melissa Stewart

Land Forms and Geology
Land and Water: Landforms & Bodies of Water by Eve Heidi Bine-Stock
The Street Beneath My Feet by Charlotte Guillain
Water Land: Land and Water Forms Around the World by Christy Hale
Hottest, Coldest, Highest, Deepest by Steve Jenkins
Introducing Landforms by Bobbie Kalman
What Shapes the Land? by Bobbie Kalman
Kaboom! A Volcano Erupts by Jessica Kulekjian
Earthshake: Poems from the Ground Up by Lisa Westberg Peter
Under Your Feet… Soil, Sand and Everything Underground by Wenjia Tang

Life Cycles
The Amazing Life Cycle of Butterflies by Kay Barnham
The Amazing Life Cycle of Plants by Kay Barnham

Life Cycles with the Very Hungry Caterpillar (board book series) by Eric Carle

Life Cycles: Everything from Start to Finish (DK Life Cycles)

A Frog's Life by Nancy Dickmann

Plant Life Cycles (A True Book: Incredible Plants!) by Mara Grunbaum

The Lost Drop: Cycles of Life by Grégoire Laforce

Animals and Plant Life Cycles: Science Lesson for Kids by Kimberly Perigard

From Tadpole to Frog (Let's-Read-and-Find-Out Science 1) by Wendy Pfeffer

Watch It Grow: Backyard Life Cycles by Barbara Reid

Rosa Explores Life Cycles by Jessica Spanyol

Life of a Honey Bee: A Book about the Life Cycle of Honey Bees by YFG Kidz

Light
Light Waves by David A. Adler

Lights Day and Night: The Science of How Light Works by Susan Hughes

Light Speaks by Christine Layton

Light: Shadows, Mirrors, and Rainbows by Natalie M. Rosinsky

All About Light (Rookie Read About Science) by Lisa Trumbauer

Maps and Mapping
My Map Book by Sara Fanelli

North, South, East, and West by Meg Greve

Keys and Symbols on Maps by Meg Greve

Mapping Penny's World by Loreen Leedy

Follow That Map! by Scot Ritchie

Me On the Map by Joan Sweeney

My Town by Rebecca Treays

Ocean
A Night at Hideaway Cove by Brenda Boreham

Hideaway Cove by Brenda Boreham

The Street Beneath My Feet by Charlotte Guillain

Journey to the Midnight Zone by Shari Last

Ocean! Waves for All by Stacy McAnulty

Hello, World! Ocean Life by Jill McDonald

Over and Under the Waves by Kate Messner

Plants and Seeds
A Seed Is Sleepy by Dianne Hutts Aston

Plant by Annabelle Griffin

Plant the Tiny Seed by Christine Matheson

Seeds Move! by Robin Page

A Seed Is the Start by Melissa Stewart

Rocks and Minerals
A Rock Is Lively by Dianna Hutts Aston

I'm Trying to Love Rocks by Bethany Barton

If You Find a Rock by Peggy Christian

My Book of Rocks and Minerals: Things to Find, Collect, and Treasure by Dennie Devin

Rocks, Fossils, and Arrowheads by Laura Evert

Let's Go Rock Collecting by Roma Gans

Animated Science: Rocks and Minerals by John Farndon

What Can You Do With A Rock? by Pat Zieltow Miller

Rocks: Hard, Soft, Smooth, and Rough by Mandy Ross

Learning About Rocks by Mari Schuh

National Geographic Everything Rocks and Minerals by Steve Tomecek

National Geographic Readers: Rocks and Minerals by Kathleen Zoehfeld

Simple Machines
Simple Machines: Wheels, Levers, and Pulleys by David A. Adler

Operation Cupcake: How Simple Machines Work by Bambi Edlund

Simple Machines (Rookie Read About Science) by Allan Fowler

Simple Machines! With 25 Science Projects for Kids by Anita Yasuda

Structures and Buildings
Up, Up, Skyscraper by Anastasia Suen

Iggy Peck, Architect by Andrea Beatty

The Story of Buildings: From the Pyramids to the Sydney Opera House and Beyond by Patrick Dillon & Stephen Biesty

How a House Is Built by Gail Gibbons

Dreaming Up by Christy Hale

Skyscraper by Jorey Hurley

Skyscrapers!: Super Structures to Design & Build by Carol A. Johmann

Look at that Building! A First Book of Structure by Scot Ritchie

Architecture According to Pigeons by Speck Lee Tailfeather

Trees, Forest and Interconnectedness
Little Tree and the Wood Wide Web by Hannah Abbo

Stand Like a Cedar by Nicola I. Campbell

What Do You See When You Look at a Tree? by Emma Carlisle

Redwoods by Jason Chin

Tall, Tall Tree: A Nature Book for Kids About Forest Habitats – A Rhyming Counting Book by Anthony D. Fredericks

The Magic and Mystery of Trees by Jen Green

Listen to the Language of the Trees: A Story of How Forests Communicate Underground by Tera Kelley

Tree Math: See, Think and Wonder by Deanna Pecaski McLennan

The Glorious Forest That Fire Built by Ginny Neil

The Busy Tree by Jennifer Ward

Be Thankful for Trees: A Tribute to the Many & Surprising Ways Trees Relate to Our Lives by Harriet Ziefert

Water Access, Conservation, and Protection

One Turtle's Last Straw: The Real-Life Rescue That Sparked a Sea Change by Elisa Boxer

A Cool Drink of Water by Barbara Cooley

Why Should I Save Water? by Jen Green

The Last Straw: Kids vs. Plastics by Susan Hood

Autumn Peltier, Water Warrior by Carole Lindstrom

We Are the Water Protectors by Carole Lindstrom

The Sea Book (Conservation for Kids) by Charlotte Milner

Ducks Overboard!: A True Story of Plastic in Our Oceans by Markus Motum

Join the No-Plastic Challenge!: A First Book of Reducing Waste by Scot Ritchie

The Water Walker by Joanne Robertson

The Last Plastic Straw: A Plastic Problem and Finding Ways to Fix It by Dee Romito

One Well: The Story of Water on Earth by Rochelle Strauss

Water Cycle

All the Water in the World by George Ella Lyon

Ocean! Waves for All by Stacy McAnulty

Over and Under the Waves by Kate Messner

Drop: An Adventure Through the Water Cycle by Emily Kate Moon

Water Is Water: A Book About the Water Cycle by Miranda Paul

The Water Cycle at Work by Rebecca Jean Olien

Hey, Water! by Antoinette Portis

Water by Melissa Stuart

The Snowman and the Sun by Susan Taghdis

Content-Rich Interactive Read-Alouds

"Reading aloud makes readers. Reading aloud makes writers. Reading aloud changes lives."
— Kate DiCamillo

There is no shortage of research that confirms that reading aloud to children is one of most beneficial activities for building knowledge, language, and engagement. In my workshops, I continually encourage teachers to read aloud every day to their students, no matter what grade they teach. As I mentioned earlier, when surveying teachers at workshops, most admit that the majority of books they choose to read aloud in their classrooms are fiction. Yet, research shows clear benefits of interactive content-rich read-alouds on young children's content vocabulary (e.g., Smolkin and Donovan, 2001), print knowledge (e.g., Justice & Piasta, 2012), and content knowledge (Strachan, 2015).

Class read-alouds can, of course, be used for the sheer pleasure of a great book: teacher reads; students listen. (I still remember the books my Grade 6 teacher read aloud to us—my favorite part of the day!) But read-alouds can also be used as teaching tools for modeling and engaging students in thinking and talking about the text. Interactive read-alouds are just that—interactive! Various interactions occur during an interactive read-aloud:

- Teacher interacting with the text
- Teacher interacting with the students
- Students interacting with the text
- Students interacting with the teacher
- Students interacting with each other

That's a lot of interacting! And adding content-rich texts into the interactive read-alouds multiplies the benefits. When we read content-rich books aloud, our students are able to engage with more complex ideas and vocabulary than what they are able to read themselves, giving them the tools to build the knowledge they need to engage with more sophisticated texts in the future. During interactive content-rich read-alouds, we can scaffold students' understanding and support their learning of new concepts by asking questions before, during, and after reading, helping them make connections between the book and their own lives or world, and extending their responses. In addition, a content-rich read-aloud can help level the literacy playing field in your classroom, allowing students who either are not print-ready or are unable to access text independently an opportunity to engage in knowledge building, meaning-making, and active discussions. A struggling decoder is not necessarily a struggling thinker. By regularly engaging in content-rich read-alouds, we provide equitable opportunities for every student to benefit from the experience.

The more we can share the fascinating world of wonder and intrigue through content-rich books with every student, the greater their success not only in building new knowledge, but also in comprehending it. Just think about it—one nonfiction read-aloud can utilize all those skills? Now, that's a substantial payoff, don't you agree?

Literacy-Rich Discussions

All classrooms involve some element of talk, but not all talk is equal. Students talking with friends in class about video game levels, weekend hockey games, or recent TikTok posts does little to support learning, but it does confirm two important things: 1) kids like to talk, and 2) kids talk at length about things they are interested in.

Talk matters. It matters in a classroom, because the voices of the children in the class engage learning, build communication, and enhance the class community. Children need multiple opportunities every day in class to practice sharing their ideas, asking questions, and communicating their thinking. Classroom discussions provide essential opportunities for learners to clarify and extend their thinking, build and strengthen their knowledge, and develop language skills—all key factors in literacy development.

In many classrooms, writing is often the go-to thinking partner; that is, we often use writing as a way for students to express their thoughts and ideas about a subject. We might read a story and then ask students to respond by writing a connection, inference, or question they might have about it. We then evaluate their thinking by assessing their written response. But written output is rarely a reflection of cognitive ability. So while we think we are assessing students' thinking, we are, in fact, assessing their ability to write. And we all know the problem that creates: students who struggle with written output are instantly put at a disadvantage. Solution? Less inking means more thinking! Replace some written-response activities with class discussions following a content lesson or nonfiction read-aloud; students are more likely to be able to focus on their thinking and communicating skills when the paper and pencils are removed. In addition, a move away from written responses can, once again, level the playing field in the classroom, removing the burden of written output from those who might be challenged by that form of communicating.

One important thing to note is the importance of helping your students develop an appropriate vocabulary for talking about their thinking before expecting them to launch into rich, engaging conversations. Heavy emphasis is

Content-rich interactive read-alouds support
- knowledge building
- "brain reading" (thinking)
- vocabulary development
- listening comprehension
- oral language
- class discussions
- student interest and engagement

"When curriculum concepts are shared and discussed over time through multiple interactive read-alouds on the same topic, they become internalized for children as they make the knowledge their own and integrate it within their existing framework." — Stephanie Strachan

We all know that some students are always engaged in class discussions, while others sit in silence. One strategy I developed to engage everyone in the class in the discussion is the Think for 1, Talk for 2, Share for 3 strategy (see page 24). It's an easy and time efficient way to way to scaffold student's thinking through oral language.

being put on the importance of integrating more oral language in literacy lessons and, while I am in agreement, I know that, unless children have developed the appropriate vocabulary—in this case, the language of thinking—and the context behind the words, the oral language will not be effective. It's like being expected to participate in a football game when you have no knowledge of the terminology or concept of the game. You might run around the field with the other players and pretend, but your skills will not develop until you have developed not only the language of game, but also the context and purpose of the game.

While one could argue that this approach could be seen as not equitable for students whose first language is not English or for those who don't like to speak in front of others, think about this: a student who is not a strong writer is not going to improve their writing by watching their classmates write because, simply put, they can't read the writing in live time. But a student who might not be a strong oral communicator can improve their oral communication skills by listening to their classmates talk, because they can hear what their peers are saying. If you build rich discussions into your daily lessons, your more reluctant communicators are surrounded by their peers sharing thinking, even if they are not actively participating themselves. By listening to talk in a classroom that has a positive, safe, and engaging community, these students just might gain the confidence and inspiration they need to join in.

5 Nudging Learning

You are now well on your way to developing powerful thinkers in your classroom by

- bringing more content-rich texts into your classroom
- choosing content-rich texts for interactive read-alouds, both in your literacy lessons and your content-area classes
- modeling learning alongside your students during your read-alouds
- engaging your students in rich discussions before, during, and after the read-alouds
- showing excitement about learning new things about the world when you share information books
- gathering text sets of engaging nonfiction books connected to your units of study, and displaying the books in the classroom for students to access
- encouraging students to choose information books for independent or partner reading

But if we truly want to nudge students' thinking and stretch their understanding, we need to (drumroll, please…) TEACH! In this chapter, I share some simple, practical lessons and strategies you can use to help your students build knowledge and nudge their thinking before, during, and after your content-rich interactive read-alouds. These strategies can be used for any grade level and with any text. You can use them for whole-class, small-group, or independent work, and they can be done completely orally, with you recording student responses, or using the templates provided for independent work. The goal of these lessons is to help your students engage with the content of the text, build knowledge and vocabulary, and stretch their thinking beyond the literal facts.

This chart might help you to determine what stage of the reading process each lesson is most suited for and to focus on one stage and lesson or strategy per read-aloud.

LESSON ROAD MAP

STAGE AND PURPOSE	Pre-Reading introduction to nonfiction texts and text structures	Before Reading building background knowledge	During Reading nudging thinking	After Reading summarizing and a final nudge
LESSONS	• What Is Nonfiction?, page 58 • Introducing Nonfiction Text Structures, page 60	• One-Word, page 66 • Book Bites, page 67	• Knew–New, page 71 • Fact–React, page 75	• One-Word, page 66 • Gisting, page 82 • What? So What? Now What?, page 84

Pre-Reading Lessons

Lesson: What Is Nonfiction?

You can find more information, booklists, and lessons on nonfiction reading in my book *Nonfiction Reading Power* (2008).

For this lesson you will need to source pairs of fiction and nonfiction texts on similar topics: e.g., *The Very Busy Spider* by Eric Carl and a nonfiction book about spiders; *Owl Babies* by Martin Wadell and a nonfiction book about owls. Your teacher-librarian will likely be able to help you with this.

Before making the shift to engaging your students with more content-rich nonfiction books, we should never assume they know what the term *nonfiction* means and how nonfiction and fiction texts compare. This lesson is to help students develop a clear understanding of the concept of nonfiction and how it compares to fiction texts. I recommend teaching it early in the school year.

- Begin the lesson by holding up a pair of books, one fiction and one nonfiction:

  I have brought in two books to show you today. I'm going to hold them up and would like you to look carefully at the covers. Think for a moment what you notice about these two books. How are they the same and how are they different? Let's start with this one

  (hold up the fiction book)

- Hold open some of the pages so students can see. Ask students what they notice about the book. (*It's about owls; it has pictures that someone drew; it's a story; the owls are talking; beginning–middle–end; have to read every page in sequence*)
- Explain that this book is a story and that another name for story is *fiction*. Write the word *Fiction* on the left side of a T-chart on chart paper or white board.
- Explain that someone wrote this story about three baby owls who are worried their mother can't find them. Tell them we can tell it's not true because the owls are talking in the story and owls can't really talk. (The author was definitely using his imagination pocket when he wrote this story!)
- Record some information under the Fiction heading (see sample T-chart below).
- Hold up the nonfiction book. Open it and show some of the pages. Ask students what they notice about this book and how it might be different from the fiction book. (*It's also about owls; it has photographs; it's true; it has a table of contents, headings, maps, some charts, lots of facts; don't have to read every page*)
- Tell students that this book is an information book, sometimes called *nonfiction*. Record the word *Nonfiction* on the top of the right side of the T-chart. Record observations down the right side of the chart (see sample T-chart below).
- Explain that the word *fiction* means "story," so *nonfiction* actually means "not a story"! Nonfiction is any type of writing that is real or true—it could even be a menu, a newspaper, a shopping list, or a recipe book.

Sample Fiction/Nonfiction T-Chart

FICTION	NONFICTION	
• *Story*	• *Facts*	
• *Characters*	• *Information*	
• *Setting*	• *Text Features:*	*Photographs*
• *Talking or dialogue:* "Hello," said Clifford.		*Labels*
• *Feelings*		*Captions*
• *Use of "I," "we," "she," "he"*		*Headings*
• *Beginning–Middle–End*		*Charts*
		Fact Boxes

- Ask students why someone might want to read a fiction story. (*They want to laugh or be entertained; they like the author; they like that type of story, e.g., mystery, adventure*)
- Ask students why someone might want to read a nonfiction text. (*They want to learn about something; they are searching for information; they are interested in the topic*)
- Take a class survey. Who prefers fiction? Nonfiction? Both? Tell students that you will be reading a lot of both stories and information books in the class this year so everyone will enjoy reading what they like!
- Pass out copies the Fiction Is/Nonfiction Is template on page 64. Place an enlarged copy of the template on the whiteboard or chart stand. Tell students that they are going to imagine they are authors writing about an animal. Explain that they will be choosing an animal to star in their books: one book is a fiction story and the other is nonfiction.
- Model with an animal (e.g., polar bear). If they are familiar with the concept of Brain Pockets, tell them to go into their imagination pocket and imagine what a polar bear might look like or be doing in a fiction story. Remind them that a fiction story is made up, so the polar bear can be doing anything and wearing anything (*driving a car, juggling, sleeping in a bed*, etc.).
- Draw an imaginary picture of the animal on the right side of the chart. Below the drawing, write a few descriptors of fiction text: *story, not true, imagination*.
- Ask students what a polar bear might look like in a nonfiction book (*more realistic, maybe on an iceberg or eating a fish, no clothes or imaginary things*).
- Draw a more realistic bear on the left side of the chart. Below the drawing, record a few words: *true, facts, information*.
- Invite students to share their animal and picture ideas with a partner before going to their desk to start their work.

Grade 1 Sample

Depending on grade level, you might want to also include the in-between type of books in this discussion; e.g., historical fiction. In this type of book, an author might use a true event in their story—e.g., the COVID outbreak—but their characters are made-up.

- Remind students that there are all kinds of different texts we can read: some are fiction, stories that are not true but that we enjoy for the imaginative ideas they give us; some are nonfiction, true information that we read to learn about the world around us. Fiction and nonfiction books look different and give readers different reading experiences.

Lesson: Introducing Nonfiction Text Structures

Text structures refer to the way authors organize information in text. Fiction texts, regardless of genre, are written using a single text structure: narrative. Most elementary students are familiar with narrative, or story structure (setting, character, plot, beginning–middle–end, problem–solution, ending), because they have likely had more exposure to fiction than nonfiction in their early reading development. Nonfiction texts are written using a variety of different structures, depending on their purpose: descriptive, persuasive, instructional, explanatory, comparative, etc. Research shows that, when readers can identify and recognize the structure of a text, their comprehension and retention of information can significantly improve (Anderson & Pearson, 1984; Kendeou & van den Broek, 2007; Meyer & Rice, 1984).

From Survey Books to a World of Nonfiction

When I was younger, I used to think all nonfiction books were information books: books that provided a reader with facts about a particular topic. Whether you were reading about sharks, bumblebees, or Japan, nonfiction books gave you the facts. Fiction books, on the other hand were widely known to offer readers different choices, based on interest and genre: realistic fiction, adventure, mystery, SF, romance, etc. This misinterpretation of nonfiction being "facts and nothing but the facts" could have been partly due to the type of nonfiction books that were available for readers at that time. Up until around the 1990s, children's book publishers were producing just one kind of nonfiction—traditional nonfiction:

> These survey books, sometimes called "all about" books, provide a general overview of a topic and are often published in large series. They emphasize balance and breadth of coverage, have an expository writing style that explains, describes, or informs, and feature language that's clear, concise, and straightforward. (Melissa Stewart, 5 Kinds of STEM-themed Nonfiction Books for Kids, 2018)

Thankfully, nonfiction books for young readers have undergone exciting and dramatic changes over the past 30 years. The all-about books have been equally matched with a wide range of information books written for different purposes and with different text structures: how-to books (instruction), why-and-how books (explanation), compare-and-contrast books (comparison), and convince-me books (persuasion). Establishing the concept of text structure early in the school year will also help your students, not only when it comes to different kinds of writing and having a clear frame in which to work, but also when you are doing read-alouds of nonfiction books. Being able to identify the text structure of a read-aloud while reading will help students with their comprehension and help them better retain the information.

For this lesson you will need
- a collection of fiction books (picture book, beginning chapter book, novel) and a few nonfiction books with each of the following text structures: description, instruction, persuasion, comparison, explanation, and biography. If you are not able to bring in actual books, you could prepare PowerPoint slides for each type of text structure.
- if possible, images of different kinds of building structures (e.g., house and skyscraper), projected so all can see

- Review the difference between fiction and nonfiction texts from the lesson on page 58 (*Fiction is a story that someone imagined; nonfiction is information that is true or real*).
- Tell students you are going to be exploring fiction and nonfiction texts a little more closely in this lesson, and you have brought some books to help you.

- Ask students if they have ever seen a building being built, maybe a new house in their neighborhood or a big skyscraper downtown. Share images, if possible, on the screen.
- Explain that when a building is being constructed, no matter what kind of building it is, they always start with a very solid frame.

  It might be a house frame or a skyscraper frame, but all buildings start with that very solid frame. When the structure is solid, then the rest of the building is added— the doors, the walls, the windows, and finally the paint and furniture. When the building is finished, you can't see the frame anymore. BUT if the frame is not solid, the building will soon start to fall apart.

- Project or hold up images of different building structures.

  Now, why am I talking about buildings when I want to be talking about books? Well, books have frames too! We can't actually see them, but every type of writing has a different frame or structure. When an author decides to write, one of the first things they do is decide what kind of frame or structure they are going to use. The text structure is how an author organizes their ideas into their writing. Let's take a closer look!

- Hold up the fiction books (picture book, chapter book, novel). Explain that these are all fiction books from the fiction side of the library. Even though they are all different stories, they all have something in common. Invite students to guess what they all share (*setting, character, beginning–middle–end, problem– solution, ending*).
- Explain that this is called the *story structure* or *narrative*—the frame of a story.

  When an author decides they want to write a story, they use this frame to help them organize their ideas. All stories look different on the outside, like houses do, but they share the same structure.

- Continue the lesson:

  Now let's look at some nonfiction books.

- Hold up examples of books that are description of a single topic and name the topic: e.g., "This book is all about bears, this book is about all spiders, and this book is about all Japan."
- Explain that even though these nonfiction books are about different topics, they all share the same frame or structure. Ask students to share what they think the structure is.

  These books are called "description" or "all-about" books. The author has picked a topic and is telling all about it. The frame a writer uses for all-about books looks like this: WHAT-WHAT-WHAT-WHAT-WHAT?

  (Share examples)

  All about Bears: WHAT does it look like? WHAT does it eat? WHAT is its habitat? WHAT are its enemies? WHAT is its life cycle?

All about Japan: WHAT is the land like? WHAT are the people like? WHAT is the government? WHAT are the cultural celebrations? WHAT is the climate?

- Next, hold up the examples of a few different instructional texts: e.g., how to draw, how to bake, how to do origami, how to play soccer, etc. Ask students if they think the books are nonfiction (*yes!*). Ask them if they think they are all-about books (*no*). Ask them what they have in common (*they tell the reader how to do something*). Tell students that how-to books are sometimes called "instructional text." The structure or frame for instruction or how-to writing is WHAT? WHAT? HOW? (*What* is the task? *What* do you need? *How* do you do it?)
- Continue sharing the different types of nonfiction texts, one structure at time. Begin to create a text structure anchor chart and record the information as you share and discuss the remaining examples of nonfiction structures.

Fiction Text Structure	Nonfiction Text Structures
Narrative • Setting • Characters • Beginning–Middle–End • Problem–Solution • Ending	**Description:** *WHAT? WHAT? WHAT? WHAT? WHAT?* **Instruction:** *WHAT? WHAT? HOW?* **Persuasion:** *WHAT? WHY? WHY? WHY? WHAT WAS THAT AGAIN?* **Comparison:** *BOTH. SAME. DIFFERENT. END* **Explanation:** *HOW? WHAT? SEQUENCE. SUMMARY. SHOW!* **Biography:** *WHO? WHAT? WHERE? WHEN? HOW? WOW!*

- Invite students to reflect on what they learned about fiction and nonfiction texts. Guide them to identify the following key points:

  - Every kind of writing starts with a text structure.
  - Text structure helps a writer organize or frame their ideas.
  - If your text structure is not strong, your writing will fall apart.
  - Fiction has one structure called *narrative*.
  - Nonfiction has six different structures: description, instruction, persuasion, comparison, explanation, and biography.

- Tell students that knowing what the text structure or frame is when they are reading can help them better make sense of the story or information.

- Optional: Pass out the Nonfiction Text Structures template on page 65 and invite students to draw book covers and titles of nonfiction books for each structure. You might want to model a few examples of this before students begin.

For more lessons and information about nonfiction text structure and writing, see my book *Nonfiction Writing Power* (2014).

Name: _____

Nonfiction Text Structures

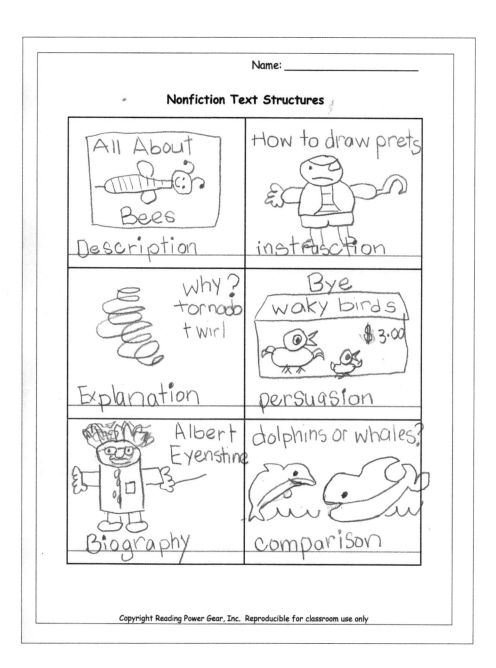

Fiction Is/Nonfiction Is

Name: _____

Choose an animal. Draw a picture of what the animal might look like in a FICTION book and what it might look like in a NONFICTION book.

Fiction is…	Nonfiction is…

Nonfiction Text Structures

Name: _____

<table>
<tr><td></td><td></td></tr>
<tr><td></td><td></td></tr>
<tr><td></td><td></td></tr>
</table>

Before-Reading Lessons

Lesson: One Word

Select a nonfiction book connected to a unit of study you are exploring with your students. Read through the book and choose one word that, for you, captures the big idea of the text. With fiction, this is often the word associated with the theme of the story; with nonfiction, it is most often the topic.

The One Word activity was originally developed for teaching the Transform strategy in the second edition of *Reading Power*. It is a practical way of helping students see how sometimes a book can change (transform) the way we think about something. I originally used fiction books for the One Word activity, but recently began exploring the idea of using it with nonfiction texts connected to Social Studies or Science. This lesson works well as a starting point to a new unit, but can also be used throughout your unit of study.

- Tell students you will be sharing a book with them shortly, but before you show them the book, you want them to do a little thinking.
- Write the one word on the whiteboard or chart stand, or use the template on page 69. Invite students to look at the word and think about it. I like to use the Think for 1, Talk for 2, Share for 3 strategy (page 24).
- Ask students to think about the word by doing three things in their minds:

    1. make a connection
    2. visualize
    3. ask a question (with fiction books I have students find a feeling)

- Give students a few minutes to think, then invite them to share their thinking with a partner.
- After a few minutes, ask some students to share out with the class. Record their thoughts around the word, on the whiteboard or chart, creating a word web.
- When the web is complete, explain that the book you will be sharing is connected to the word.
- While you are reading, tell students to pay attention to their thinking and notice if anything starts to stretch or transform.
- After reading, revisit the word web. Ask the students to think about any new thoughts or ideas that they now have, after listening to the book.

    How has your thinking stretched?

- Again, invite students to Think for 1, Talk for 2, Share for 3 (see page 24).
- Ask some students to share their thoughts with the class.
- Using a different color marker, record the new thoughts on the same one-word web, but create an outer layer so that the new thinking stands out from the original.
- Reflect on their thinking:

    What I really liked about this lesson is how it can help us see that sometimes something we read or learn about can stretch our thinking and give us new ideas to consider. New thinking doesn't erase or replace our original thoughts, but it's valuable to know that reading can change, stretch, and transform our thinking sometimes. This book certainly did that for us, didn't it?

Matt Vautour, teacher at Quigley Elementary in Kelowna, was exploring single-use plastics with his Grade 1 class. He read the book *One Turtle's Last Straw: The Real-Life Rescue That Sparked a Sea Change* by Elisa Boxer for this One Word lesson. The notes around the outside of the web not connected by lines to the central word are written in a different color and represent students' after-reading thinking.

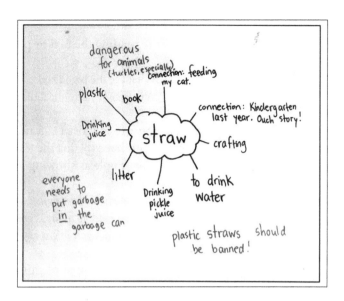

Lesson: Book Bites

Before reading a content-rich text to your class, it's important to preface the reading with a quick *bite* of background knowledge and vocabulary to help maximize student engagement and understanding. Think of it as a small appetizer to the book you are about to share! A Book Bite is a way of making the text accessible for every student by providing key ideas and vocabulary from the text to help build their knowledge with accurate information prior to reading. It is quick (no more than five minutes), but very valuable for building comprehension when reading content-rich books to your students. Book Bites work particularly well when you are engaging your students in text sets connected to a Science or Social Studies unit. Knowledge builds, as students encounter similar information and vocabulary within these text sets.

Don't Ask—Just Tell!

Back in the day, KWL (Know–Wonder–Learn) was a popular pre-reading strategy, thought to be helpful in building background knowledge. Prior to reading a nonfiction text or beginning a new unit in Science, Social Studies, or Math, the teacher would ask "What do you already know about…" and students would have an opportunity to list (or provide information for the teacher to record on a class chart) anything they already knew about the topic. While I like the idea of activating prior knowledge before reading or learning something new, the problem with KWL was that the students who knew something about the topic got to say what they knew but students who didn't know anything about it often said things that might or might not have been correct, or might not have related to what they were about to read. This "idea popping" proved challenging, because we often didn't have adequate time to sort out accurate from inaccurate, what you're going to learn from what you're not going to learn, and it resulted in more confusion building than knowledge building! Rather than asking students questions about topics they may or may not know the answers to, help build background knowledge by building background knowledge! In other words, don't ask—just tell! Book Bites is a simple pre-reading strategy that can help structure your telling before launching into the text.

See page 70 for a Book Bites Planner for your use.

In a recent webinar on Effective Reading Comprehension Instruction, presenter Dr. Shannon Vaughn, from the Education Department at University of Texas, Austin, encourages educators to help their students become word learners and word collectors because "learning vocabulary words is a lifelong endeavor." She refers to vocabulary as the "currency of reading comprehension" (or the bitcoin, before bitcoin crashed!) that strengthens a reader's understanding.

5 TIPS FOR BOOK BITES

1. Prior to reading the text or passage to your students, ask yourself:

    1. What are the big ideas?
    2. What are the key vocabulary words?

2. You can use a short (1–3 minute) YouTube video (YouTube Kids is a great resource) that explains the topic briefly. If you can't find a video, the Book Bite can be as simple as showing a photograph and talking about it:

    This is a picture of a jellyfish… and this is a picture of an iceberg. The story we are going to be reading today is going to focus on both a jellyfish and an iceberg. What are some things you might expect to find in this book?

    It takes just a couple of minutes, but the purposeful front-end loading and discussion really helps set the scene for every student.

3. Highlighting new vocabulary before reading is also important for helping students build knowledge and engagement. Never assume students know the vocabulary before you read! While it's impossible to cover every new word a student might encounter in a text, you can simplify it by asking yourself: What words are most important? (e.g., *iceberg*) What words appear again and again in the text? What words can students use to build other words? (e.g., the word *equal* is the root of many other words: *equality*, *equitable*, etc.). Try to limit your vocabulary list to five key words.

4. When introducing new vocabulary to students, it's important that they both hear and see the words, so make sure you have them visible on a whiteboard, chart stand, or screen. Provide quick, child-friendly definitions for each word, with pictures or images if applicable, and, of course, never let a new word go without providing some reference to morphology (chunking, blending, sounding out) or word-learning strategies.

5. If you are using a text set connected to a unit of study, students will begin to recognize the key vocabulary as they encounter similar words in different texts over days or weeks, helping to increase their comprehension and strengthen their knowledge building.

One Word

Look at the word and think about connections, visual images, and feelings connected to the word. Record your ideas in a web around the word.

Book Bites Planner

Book Title/ Passage Heading	
Big Idea	
Key Vocabulary	1. 2. 3. 4. 5.

Pembroke Publishers ©2024 *Powerful Thinking* by Adrienne Gear ISBN 9781551383637

During-Reading Lessons

Lesson: Knew–New

"Connecting what readers know to new information is the core of learning and understanding." — Stephanie Harvey (2007, p. 17)

If your students are not familiar with Brain Pockets, it's helpful to introduce them to this concept and visual prior to this lesson.

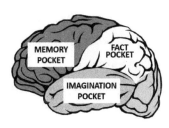

For more information about Brain Pocket Writing, see my book *Powerful Writing Structures* (2019); for more information on Brain Pocket Reading, see my book *Reading Power, Revised & Expanded Edition* (2015).

Brain Pockets

One of the main differences between making connections to fiction text and making connections to nonfiction text is the source of the reader's connections; in other words, where their connections come from. The concept of Brain Pockets originated in my book *Nonfiction Reading Power* (2007) and is intended to help students recognize the enormous value their thinking has on both reading and writing.

Introducing Brain Pockets

- Explain that our brains are the storage place for all of our thinking. Draw a simple brain shape on the whiteboard or chart stand. While you explain, draw and label the three pockets inside the brain shape (see sample in margin).

    Like files stored in a computer, our thoughts are stored inside our brains. Thousands of thoughts squished into your little brain—it's hard to imagine! Our brains have three different pockets to help organize our thoughts: our personal experiences and memories are stored in a Memory Pocket; facts and information we know are stored in a Fact Pocket; and our creative and imaginative thoughts are stored in an Imagination Pocket.

    (Note: This is not based on science by any stretch!)

- Explain that Brain Pockets are very helpful for writing. Before a writer starts writing, they need to decide what pocket they want to be in and then find their ideas for writing inside that pocket.
- Explain that Brain Pockets are also helpful for making connections when we read:

    If I'm reading a story about two friends who get into an argument, I might go into my memory pocket and think, "That reminds me of when my friend and I had an argument". If I'm reading an information book about owls, I might go into my fact pocket and think, "I already knew that owls sleep in the daytime".

- Explain that paying attention to the thoughts in your Brain Pockets when you read can really help you understand the story or information better.

- Share or draw a picture of Brain Pockets and invite students to name the three pockets: *Memory, Fact, and Imagination*.
- Explain that today, you will be focusing on making connections. Hopefully, most of your students will be familiar with this strategy, but it's always good to review!

    Making connections is when something in the story reminds you of something that has happened to you, or somewhere you have been, or someone you know. When you make a connection, it helps you understand the story a little better, because you have had that same experience.

When we make connections to stories, we often connect to an experience, a character, or a feeling.

(Record this on a chart stand or whiteboard)

FICTION (Memory Pocket)	NONFICTION
• *Experiences* • *Characters* • *Feelings*	

- Hold up a story and model examples of these three personal connections. Ask students what pocket they think you were finding your connections from (*Memory Pocket*).
- Hold up a nonfiction book about a planet or volcano (something students would likely not have personal experiences with):

  When we read nonfiction books like this one, it gets a little tricky. This book is about the planet Jupiter. Has anyone every been there before? (Someone always puts their hand up when I ask this!!) Are there any characters I can connect to? (no) Do I have any feelings about Jupiter? Not really. So, how can I make connections to this book?

- Point to the Brain Pockets picture. Ask students if they have any ideas about making connections to nonfiction. Explain:

  When we are reading nonfiction or information books, we need to move into our Fact Pockets to find our connections! When we make connections to information, the best thing to do is to connect to things you already know about the topic. We call this "connecting to background knowledge." And your background knowledge is stored in your Fact Pocket! We might not be able to find facts in our Fact Pocket connected to the topic, but that is okay. For example, I don't know very much about the planet Jupiter, so I might not be able to make too many connections. But I can always put new facts into my fact pocket.

- Explain that sometimes, depending on the topic we are reading about, we can make connections to experiences. For example, if you are reading an information book about owls and you remember when the owl rescue officer came to school and brought a real owl, you would have connections to an experience.
- Add points to the chart in the Nonfiction column.

FICTION (Memory Pocket)	NONFICTION (Fact Pocket)
• *Experiences* • *Characters* • *Feelings*	• *Background knowledge* • *Things I already know about the topic* • *Experiences*

- Write the words *Knew* and *New* on the board in a T-chart. Discuss the two words and what they mean.

Knew	New
•	•
•	•
•	•

- Explain that Knew–New is a helpful way to make connections when you read information. While you read, you can think to yourself, "*Is this something I already KNEW or is this a NEW fact I can add to my Fact Pocket?*"
- Choose a nonfiction book, or a page from a book, to read aloud. Explain that you are going to be reading the passage slowly, one sentence at a time. After each sentence, you will consider if the information you just read is something you already knew or if it was a new fact.
- Read and talk through the text, recording facts on either side of the Knew–New chart. For example,

   "Tarantulas are the largest spiders." Now I knew that tarantulas were big, but I didn't realize they were the largest spiders. So, I'm going to write that fact on the New side.

- End the lesson:

   Today we have been learning about background knowledge and how it can help us when we read information books. Here, on the Knew side, are facts I already knew about tarantulas, but on the New side are new facts that I can add to my Fact Pocket. The next time I'm reading about tarantulas, I will have more background knowledge to connect to!

LESSON EXTENSION: INDEPENDENT KNEW–NEW

Students can practice the Knew–New strategy when they are reading independently. I like to give them four to six sticky notes (half for Knew; the other half for New) to stick onto the pages of the information book while they read. Older students can record a fact on the sticky note (see sample). Afterward, students can pull off the sticky notes and stick them onto the Let's Do the Knew–New template on page 79.

Warning! There are always students who like to claim, "I knew that" for every fact you share. While your thinking voice might be saying "No, you didn't," remember the focus of this lesson is for students to gain an awareness and understanding of background knowledge—where it's located and how we build it. No matter what side of the chart the fact is recorded on, in the end, it all becomes "Now, I KNOW!"

Grade 2 New–Knew sample
New: "Bats drink nector"
Knew: "Bats sleep upside down"

Students love making Knew–New connections! I am not sure whether it's the catchy name or the fact that most are able to successfully identify at least one fact they already knew and one new fact. I often use this strategy orally when reading information books aloud. It's quick, it's simple, and it really helps students pay attention to their thinking. Before reading, tell the students to pay attention to their Fact Pocket and facts they already knew, and to new facts. Use the Think for 1, Talk for 2, Share for 3 strategy (page 24) for students to think, talk, and share their Knew–New.

Optional: After sharing their Knew-News connections orally, students can record their Knew–New connections on any of the Knew–New templates on pages 77–78.

Grade 2 Knew–New connections to the book *Not a Buzz to be Found: Insects in Winter* by Linda Glasser

Kindergarten New–Knew connections to the book *Caterpillar to Butterfly* by Laura Marsh

Lesson: Fact–React

One of the most important things we can do to help our students develop as thinkers is consistently remind them to turn on their thinking!

- Share the image below or draw a similar one. Ask students what they think it means.

Adapted from "information vs knowledge" gapingvoid.com

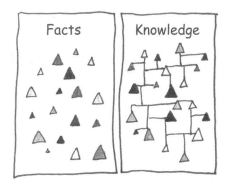

- Discuss the fact that the visual helps us understand the difference between facts and knowledge. Facts just sit alone, but when you add your thinking to the facts, the facts come together and it helps you understand them better. (I love this image!)
- This is what I tell students (of course, feel free to make it your own!):

  When I was in school (a hundred years ago!) all I ever did in Science and Social Studies classes was to find facts, memorize them, and give them back to my teacher. I was very good at memorizing facts, and I thought that the more facts I could squish in my head, the smarter I would be. Wrong! Facts are important, yes, but a fact is just a fact until we add our thinking to it. When you memorize facts without adding your thinking, the facts often disappear after a while. What's more important than memorizing facts is to wonder, connect, visualize, infer—in other words, to react to the fact with our thinking. That's what turns ordinary information into meaningful knowledge!

- Tell students you are going to share a book that is filled with interesting facts. First, students will gather facts, then they will have a chance to react to each fact by adding their thinking to it, so that the facts become more meaningful.
- Create a large two-column chart and write *Fact* on one side and *React* on the other.
- Begin reading a short passage from a nonfiction text, possibly related to a unit of study. Pause after one or two sentences and invite students to identify one important fact. Record the fact in the Fact column.
- Remind students that the facts are important, but so is our thinking. On the right side of the table, record your thinking in the React column. Invite students to share their reactions to the facts and record them on the chart.
- Use the Fact–React 1 template on page 80, or the Fact–React 2 template on page 81 for early primary students, if you want students to record their own responses independently or in partners. Because there are often multiple facts in these books, students can select a few to record on their page.

I have had great success with this lesson using the book *Lifetime: Amazing Numbers in Animal Lives* by Lola M. Schaefer.

Gr. 2 Fact–React sample using the book *Heads and Tails Insects* by John Canty

Fact (information from the book)	React (knowledge from my brain)
Male seahorses lay 1000 babies in their lifetime.	WOW! I never knew male seahorses had babies! Do any other male creatures have babies? 1000! That's a LOT of seahorses!

Fact	Reaction
1. • waSps chew there food	• I din't Know that waSps could chew-like us
2. • HoneYbees wings beat 200 times per second	• I can't See that in my mind.
3. • a insect has a skeleton out side there bodys!	• I think I'd rather have bones.
4. • there are 900,000 Kinds of iNsects	• I wonder how many kinds of Snakes there are?
Name	Great thinking! ★

RECOMMENDED ANCHOR BOOKS FOR FACT–REACT

Heads and Tails Insects by John Canty

Good Trick, Walking Stick! by Sheri Mabry Bestor

I See Sea Food: Sea Creatures That Look Like Food by Jenna Grodzicki

What Do You Do When Someone Wants to Eat You? by Steve Jenkins (or any book by him!)

Do Frogs Drink Hot Chocolate? How Animals Keep Warm by Etta Kaner

Supermoms! by Heather Lang

All the Birds in the World by David Opie

Packs by Hannah Salyer

The Search for the Gigantic Arctic Jellyfish by Chloe Savage

Lifetime: The Amazing Numbers in Animal Lives by Lola M. Schaefer

Tree Hole Homes by Melissa Stewart

Summertime Sleepers by Melissa Stewart

Steve the Dung Beetle on a Roll by Susan R. Stoltz

Knew–New Connections 1

Name: _____

KNEW I already knew…	NEW This is new to me:

Knew–New Connections 2

Name: _____

Title: _____ Author: _____

I already KNEW…	This is NEW to me:
I visualized…	I'm wondering…

Name: _____

Let's Do the Knew-New!

I already KNEW...	This is NEW!

Pembroke Publishers ©2024 *Powerful Thinking* by Adrienne Gear ISBN 9781551383637

Fact–React 1

Name: _____

Fact (from the text)	React (from my thinking)

Pembroke Publishers ©2024 *Powerful Thinking* by Adrienne Gear ISBN 9781551383637

Name: _____

Fact-React 2

Fact (from the text)	React (from my thinking)

After-Reading Lessons

Lesson: Gisting

While I recognize that the main goal of this book is to help students move beyond a literal understanding of content material and focus on building knowledge and stretching thinking, the bottom line is that identifying the main idea or summarizing information is necessary before the stretch can occur. Information books are full of so much information that students often have a difficult time sorting through it all. Determining importance or identifying the gist of a piece of text has proven to be challenge for many learners. Some readers, when asked to summarize, leave out all the important points and focus on details that, while interesting, aren't necessarily connected to the main idea. Others go on and on and on (aka TMI), adding irrelevant information and making the summary longer than the original text! Looking back on my old university textbooks and seeing pages and pages of highlighted paragraphs (yes, paragraphs!), it is clear that I, too, never learned how to effectively determine what was most important! Without the ability to determine what the main point of a text is, the gist of it, a student has little or no chance of nudging their thinking into more interactive and insightful layers of comprehension. So, how can do we support them? My answer (as always)—make it simple!

In my book *Nonfiction Reading Power*, I outline several strategies for helping students determine the important or big ideas in an informational text, including Key Words, Sum it Up, and Sketch Summary (see *Nonfiction Reading Power* pages 87–100). For this book, I have discovered a new quick, effective strategy called *Gisting* (based on a webinar by Sharon Vaughn) that you can use to help students identify what's important after reading. This strategy focuses on two simple things: What or who is this about? and What is the most important thing about who or what?

- Begin the Lesson:

  I want you to imagine you are reading a really great information book and your friend comes over and says "Hey! What's that book about? Be quick! I have to pick up my sister!" What would you say?

  We've been exploring a lot of information books and you've probably noticed when you read information books that there is a lot of information in them! Some of the information is really important and some of it is less important, more like interesting details. Sometimes it's hard to narrow it down to just one main idea. Another name some people use for main idea is gist. *"What's the gist of this?" means "In just a few words, what is this all about?" In other words, leave out the details and just tell me the most important stuff— and make it SHORT! Today I'm going to teach you a simple way to find just the gist of the information.*

- Copy the Just the Gist! chart on the whiteboard or chart stand. Explain each step, one at a time.

Just the Gist!

1. What or Who is the most important in the text?
2. What is the most important thing ABOUT the What or Who?
3. Combine 1 and 2 and write the gist in 10 words or less!

This lesson is adapted from a webinar by Sharon Vaughn, "The Science of Reading Comprehension: Effective Reading Comprehension Instruction (#2 Spotlight)" https://www.youtube.com/watch?v=s1LHkGXfRdw&t=1s

This sample uses the first two pages of a book called *Saving the Spotted Owl: Zalea's Story* by Nicola Jones.

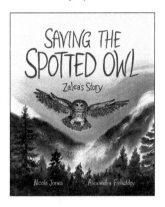

- When practicing this strategy with your students, use a collection of short passages from an information text.
- Show students the pages you will be reading from. Tell them that there is a lot of information there, but that, while you are reading, you want them to be thinking about "just the gist" of the text. Basically, you want them to try to shrink all the information into just one sentence.
- After reading, tell students that there was a lot of information there, but if someone asked them to tell them just the gist, what would they say?
- Refer to the chart. First, ask them to name the most important who or what (*Zalea, a baby owl*).
- Then, ask them to tell a partner what they think was the most important thing about Zalea (*She fell out of her tree and was rescued by scientists*). You might want to model a few details that are less important and discuss them: e.g., Zalea was three weeks old (detail), the scientists arrived on a spring day (detail), they put the owl in a box (detail).
- Finally, model how to combine the two points into one sentence that tells just the gist. Record the gist on the board: *A baby owl named Zalea fell out of her tree and was rescued by scientists.*
- Hold open the book and show the students how much information you just read—a lot! They helped you find the gist and shrink all the information into just one short sentence. Tell them they are excellent "gisters"!
- Continue practicing gist sentences with one or two more pages or paragraphs from the text. It is not necessary to read an entire book or create a huge collection of gist sentences. Just focus on three or four short paragraphs or sections, and three or four corresponding gist sentences.
- Depending on the information and your grade level, these gist sentences can later be combined to create a gisty summary. Combine the three or four gist sentences and, again depending on your grade level, add a topic and concluding sentence. Use the Just the Gist template on page 90 as a lesson guide or for students to practice independently.
- End the lesson:

> *Readers, today we have been practicing finding the gist. Finding the gist means being able to say, in just a few words, what the text is about. When we get the gist, we want to try to focus on only the most important facts from the text.*

Somebody–Wanted–But–So–Then

When helping students summarize a fictional story, I discovered a simple and effective strategy several years ago called Somebody–Wanted–But–So–Then and have never looked back! It has proven, time and time again to be the most valuable tool for helping students summarize the main events in a story, while leaving out all the unnecessary details (see summary of Goldilocks and the Three Bears below). I have even found it helpful to use as a story-planning strategy when teaching story writing.

Somebody: Who is the main character?
Wanted: What does the character want? What is their goal?

But: Who or what is preventing the character from achieving their goal? (problem)

So: Who or what helps the character achieve their goal? (solution)

Then: How does the story end?

To simplify this for early primary students, I recommend combining the last two headings—*Somebody, Wanted, But, So then*—making it a four-box organizer.

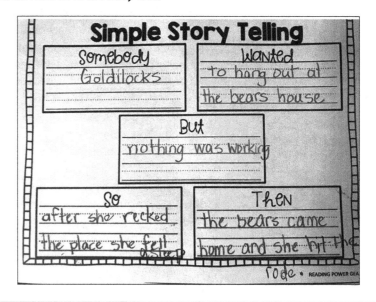

RECOMMENDED BOOKS FOR GISTING

Hottest Coldest Fastest Deepest by Steve Jenkins (Gist: Earth is filled with remarkable, extreme places)

What Do You Do When Someone Wants to Eat You? by Steve Jenkins (Gist: Animals use many different ways to protect themselves from enemies)

Saving the Spotted Owl: Zalea's Story by Nicola Jones (Gist: A baby owl named Zalea fell out of her tree and was rescued by scientists)

Hiders Seekers Finders Keepers by Jessica Kulekjian (Gist: Different animals use different ways to survive in winter)

Summertime Sleepers: Animals That Estivate by Melissa Stewart (Gist: Some animals sleep or estivate during the summer months)

Thank You, Moon: Celebrating Nature's Nightlight by Melissa Stewart (Gist: The moon helps many animals on earth in different ways)

Whale Fall: Exploring an Ocean-Floor Ecosystem by Melissa Stewart (Gist: A dead whale provides food sources for many other ocean organisms)

Lesson: What? So What? Now What?

Levels of Understanding

As many of you know and even practice, a common way of having students respond to an informational text is to ask them what the text is literally about; in other words, to summarize the gist. Don't get me wrong—a literal retell is an important skill students will need as they move into high school and, for some, post secondary studies. But what's essential to remember is that a literal summary, retell, or gist is not the end of understanding—it's the starting place. We need to think of ourselves in a perpetual state of nudging!

The chart below breaks down the levels of understanding into three phases: literal, interactive, and extended. This visual helps to illustrate our goal: nudging our students from the top of this chart to the bottom. While a literal level of understanding is important, it is not our end goal. Many students get stuck in the literal, particularly when reading informational texts, possibly because they haven't been given the opportunity to stretch their thinking beyond the facts. That is why our instructional nudging is so important. Students need us to help facilitate the stretch by carefully guiding conversations and questions toward the next level of understanding.

Don't rush. We can't expect students to extend their thinking right away. They need time and practice interacting with many different texts over many read-aloud sessions, slowly adding their thinking—their connections, questions, and inferences—to the information, with your help. Slow and steady instruction and lots of practice will ensure the greatest success!

Literal
Strategies required: summary, gist, retell, recount, main idea
↓
Interactive
Strategies required: Connect, Question, Visualize, Infer
↓
Extended
Strategies required: Transform, Synthesize, Rethink

The What? So What? Now What? strategy was developed to help you gently nudge your students away from that literal starting point of a text to the place where the deep learning and thinking takes place. We begin with *What?*, or the literal; we move to *So What?*, or the interactive; finally we arrive at *Now What?*, or extended understanding.

This lesson shows students moving through all three levels of understanding in one lesson; however, I recommend moving gradually at first. Particularly with younger learners who have not had a lot of Reading Power experience, don't rush! Spend several lessons (weeks, months even!) just practicing What? and So What? Only when you feel your students are comfortable with the first two levels and are demonstrating interactive thinking would I recommend nudging them into the extended Now What? level.

For this lesson, find an interesting, shorter passage from a book that you will be reading aloud.

- Begin the lesson:
- Remind students that when we read information, it's important to be able to identify the What? or *What is this about?*
- Create a single-column chart with the word *What?* at the top. Tell students you are going to read a short passage out loud. Their job is to listen and decide the What? or the gist of the passage. (See page 82 for a lesson on identifying the gist.)
- Read the passage aloud.

Starfish

Starfish, also known as Sea Stars, are one of the most beautiful-looking animals in the vast ocean, but they are quite unusual. First, they have a surprisingly unusual anatomy, with no brain or blood. Second, they digest their food outside their bodies, not inside like us. But likely the most unusual thing is the fact that when a starfish loses an arm, a new one grows back. This process is called regeneration. Regenerating their own arms is perhaps one of the most useful things a starfish can do. Incredibly, if the severed arm is not harmed, it can heal itself and even regenerate into a genetically identical starfish. Pretty cool, right?

- Ask students to think about two or three important facts from the passage. Invite them to Think for 1, Talk for 2, Share for 3 (see page 24).
- Record some of their responses on the chart, guiding them if they focus on a less important detail.

Starfish
What?
• *no brain or blood* • *digest food outside body* • *arms regenerate*

- Continue the lesson:

   Being able to find the important facts or the What? is an important skill, especially when we are reading information. You all did a great job doing that. But we are not done! We are just getting started. Remember, in this class, we are not just fact finders, we are thinkers! So, while I stretch this chart, I want you to stretch your thinking. I want you to think So What? about starfish. What are you wondering about them? Do you have any connections? What are you thinking about? Think for 1 minute, talk to a partner for 2, and then we will share out for 3!

- Add a second column to the right side of the chart and label it *So What?* Allow time for students to share their thinking with a partner. Invite some to share their thinking with the class while you record some of their responses.

Starfish	
What?	**So What?**
• *no brain or blood* • *digest food outside body* • *arms regenerate*	• *How many kinds of starfish are there?* • *How do they find food if they don't have a brain?* • *That reminds me of worms cuz when you cut them in half they grow again.* • *Why can't we grow new arms?*

If your students are new to this strategy, you may choose to stop the lesson here. For the purpose of this book, however, I'm going to share the next stage of this lesson, when you will nudge your students into the extended level of thinking or the Now What?

- Celebrate the great thinking students are doing. Tell them that you think they are ready to do a little more stretching. Explain that you are going to stretch the chart one more time! Add a third column and label it *Now What?* Explain that this column is for thoughts that students might now have that about starfish, but that their thinking needs to stretch away from facts about starfish to thoughts that are, perhaps, bigger.

> *Sometimes, when we read information, our thinking can go away from the actual information to something connected to it. What are you thinking now that you hadn't thought about before? How has this information about starfish and regeneration changed the way you think about something else? Now this is when you really need to consider new ideas, maybe not connected to starfish but connected to something else. Try stretching your thinking and see what happens. Think for 1, talk for 2, and then we will share out.*

Not all students will be able to do this the first time. Often, students go back to restating facts about the information. But one or two students might say something that captures a transformed thought. Those are the responses you need to home in on and really celebrate.

Starfish		
What?	**So What?**	**Now What?**
• *no brain or blood* • *digest food outside body* • *arms regenerate*	• *How many kinds of starfish are there?* • *How do they find food if they don't have a brain?* • *That reminds me of worms cuz when you cut them in half they grow again.* • *Why can't we grow new arms?*	• *Too bad that doesn't happen to soldiers. If it did, I bet soldiers wouldn't be so scared to go to war.*

The student who made this Now What? comment was a child in my class who was not reading at grade level, a struggling decoder, if you will. What this sample clearly indicates is that a struggling decoder is not always a struggling thinker. By removing the burden of the code, or doing the book reading for our students, we enable them to focus on their brain reading. And for students like this one, their thinking shines through. I'm not suggesting that this student does not need support with code—he certainly does. But if we continually focus on what students can't do, we might be limiting what they can do. This student demonstrated far deeper thinking than many of the strong decoders in the class. And if helping students stretch their thinking and deepen their learning are our goals, then moments like this are worth celebrating.

- End the lesson:

> *I'm so impressed with all of you! You really have shown some big stretches in your thinking today! Well done! Remember that reading isn't just about what is in the book. It's what is in our heads that we bring into the book that really helps bring meaning and understanding to what we are reading. Great thinking, everyone!*

LESSON EXTENSION

The What? So What? Now What? strategy can be practiced using different text sets connected to a unit of study. As always, books are your best resource to support the stretch! Using three different books that target the topic in different ways and from different lenses can really help to extend your students' thinking beyond just the literal facts. The chart on page 89 includes a trio of books connected to each unit of study. Each book represents one lesson: literal, interactive, or extended. The lessons can be done on consecutive days or interspersed throughout the unit. For independent work, students can record their thinking using the What? So What? Now What? templates (Primary on page 91; Intermediate on page 92) while you read aloud. Alternatively, your lessons can be done orally, as you read aloud and then record your students' responses onto a class chart.

Topic	What? Literal	So What? Interactive	Now What? Extended
Trees: interconnectedness of nature	*The Magic and Mystery of Trees* by Jen Green	*The Last Tree* by Maria Quintana Silva	*Luna and Me* by Jenny Sue Kostecki-Shaw
Water	*Hide-Away Cove* by Brenda Boreham	*Duffy's Lucky Escape* by Ellie Jackson	*Join the Non-Plastic Challenge* by Scot Ritchie
Earth	*Earth! My First 4.54 Billion Years* by Stacy McAnulty	*Thank-you, Earth* by April Pulley Sayre	*Be a Good Ancestor* by Leona Prince
Animal Protection/ Conservation	*Ape* by Martin Jenkins	*Ivan: The Remarkable True Story of the Shopping Mall Gorilla* by Katherine Applegate	*The Watcher: Jane Goodall's Life with Chimps* by Jeanette Winter
Community	*What Is a Community?* by Dwayne Hicks *Whose Hands Are These?* by Miranda Paul	*Look Where We Live: A First Look at Community Building* by Scot Ritchie	*Maybe Something Beautiful: How Art Transformed a Neighborhood* by F. Isabel Campoy
Rocks and Minerals	*Absolute Expert Rocks and Minerals* by Ruth Strother	*A Rock is Lively* by Dianna Hutts Aston	*Everybody Needs a Rock* by Byrd Baylor
Global Education	*This is a School* by John Schu	*School Days Around the World* by Margriet Ruurs	*The Way to School* by Rosemary McCarney
Whales	*All Things Whales For Kids* by Animal Reads (or any all-about book on whales)	*Whale Fall: Exploring an Ocean Floor Ecosystem* by Melissa Stewart	*Whales and Us: Our Shared Journey* by India Dejardins
The Moon	*Moon! Earth's Best Friend* by Stacy McAnulty	*Mi'kmaw Moons: The Seasons in Mi'kma'ki* by Cathy LeBlanc	*Thank you, Moon: Celebrating Nature's Nightlight* by Melissa Stewart
Truth and Reconciliation	*This is a School* by John Schu	*I Am Not a Number* by Kathy Kacer or *Phyllis's Orange Shirt* by Phyllis Webstad	*With Our Orange Hearts* by Phyllis Webstad

Just the Gist

Name: _____

Gisty Summary

| Gist 1 |
| Gist 2 |
| Gist 3 |
| Gist 4 |

Name: _____

What? So What? Now What? Primary

What? Fact from the text	**So What?** Thoughts from my head	**Now What?** Stretched thinking

Pembroke Publishers ©2024 *Powerful Thinking* by Adrienne Gear ISBN 9781551383637

What? So What? Now What? Intermediate

Name: _____

Title: _____ Author: _____

What? Literal Facts	So What? Connections/Questions/ Inferences	Now What? Transformed Thinking

Pembroke Publishers ©2024 *Powerful Thinking* by Adrienne Gear ISBN 9781551383637

Powerful Thinking Across the Curriculum

As I reflect on Reading Power and my work on comprehension instruction over the years, I recognize that the book *Reading Power* was a starting place for many of us who had never actually "taught" reading comprehension; I like to believe that it served and continues to serve us well. *Reading Power*, although almost 20 years old, is still being used in schools, across Canada and in small pockets of Sweden, Australia, the US, and the UK, to help students think while they read. As someone who lives in a permanent state of reflection, my stretched thinking, as well as the gist of this book, is this: If those strategies can help students develop a better understanding of what they are reading, why can't we use those same strategies and apply them to all areas of learning? Thinking is not limited to reading and can be applied to every aspect of teaching.

If our goal is help our students become powerful thinkers, thinking needs to be integrated into every aspect of our curriculum, not just in our literacy block. In this part of the book, I share ways to integrate thinking into every subject.

6 Thinking in Science

The word *science* comes from the Latin word for "knowledge"; the word *method* comes from the Greek word that means "road." So the scientific method is a road to knowledge!

Children are naturally curious about the world and eager to discover as much as they can about it. Science in school, rather than being viewed as the memorization of scientific facts, becomes a way of thinking and trying to better understand the world, and involves children engaged in the process of discovery. Let's face it, wouldn't we all rather be outside with a magnifying glass and a clipboard than inside taking notes from the whiteboard? Science is brimming with opportunities for practicing thinking. From demonstrating curiosity about the natural world, through observing objects and events, identifying questions, making connections, conducting scientific investigations, and making predictions, to transforming our understanding about the world around us, true science evolves from deep thinking and deep questions. Here are a few suggestions of ways to integrate thinking into your units of study in Science.

Wonder Walk

I love using the great outdoors to inspire students to start thinking like a scientist. Just as visualizing is at the forefront of thinking in gym class (see page 140), questioning seems to be the dominant strategy of both experienced and budding scientists. Taking your students on a Wonder Walk gives students a wonderful, open-ended exercise to practice scientific inquiry and record questions they have about something they notice or observe in nature.

Lesson: Taking a Wonder Walk

You might wish to review the difference between quick and deep-thinking questions: a quick question is one that you ask and are able to quickly find out the answer; deep-thinking questions inspire you to think more deeply because the answer is not easily found or known. For more information on quick and deep-thinking questions, see *Reading Power* 2nd edition, pages 65–70.

While there are many other Questioning books, I have tried to include only those books that focus on questions about nature and the world around us.

- Tell students they are going to practice becoming scientists today.
- Discuss what a scientist is. Explain that scientists are people who are very curious about the world around them. They are deep thinkers who try to understand how our world, or things in our world, works. They ask questions, study, and observe things carefully, sort and classify things, and come up with ideas and conclusions about them. Sometimes, they even discover something new!
- Tell students there are different kinds of scientists who study different things—scientists who like to learn about living things are called biologists; scientists who study rocks are called geologists; scientists who study animals are sometimes called zoologists.
- Explain that, today, you will be practicing becoming scientists who are curious about nature and who ask deep-thinking questions about what they observe.
- Share an anchor book (or two) that encourage and inspire deep-thinking questions. One of my old favorites is *I Wonder* by Tana Hoban; my new favorite is *What's in Your Pocket?: Collecting Nature Treasures* by Heather L. Montgomery.

Here are some anchor books to inspire deep-thinking questions about nature and the world around us.

The Boy and the Sea by Camille Andros
I Wonder by Harriet Fischel
Stella books (series) by Marie-Louise Gay
I Wonder by Tana Hoban
What's in Your Pocket?: Collecting Nature Treasures by Heather L. Montgomery
The Girl with Big, Big Questions by Britney Winn Lee
Questions, Questions by Marcus Pfister

Where Does Pepper Come From? And Other Fun Facts by Brigitte Raab
Why?: The Best Ever Question and Answer Book about Nature, Science and the World around You by Catherine Ripley
I Wonder Why by Lois Rock
Ask Me by Bernard Waber

Depending on your school location and access to nature, you may need to pre-plan your walk.

- Explain to students that they will be going on a Wonder Walk. You will be taking them on a walk outside in nature. On the walk, you want them to imagine they are scientists—looking closely, taking notice, and asking deep questions about things they see.
- Pass out the My Wonder Walk template on page 98. Clipboards are helpful, if you have them.
- When you are outside, model to students how to find a nature spot, focus on something that interests them, observe carefully, and then ask some deep questions.

Students, I've decided to pause here in front of this tree. I like trees and this one caught my eye because of the pattern of deep crevasses in the trunk. I think it would be a good nature spot for me to observe and wonder. First, I'm going to start with looking carefully at the tree. I'm noticing the bark, the grayish color of the bark, and the interesting lines the bark is making. I see a little ant crawling up the tree here. I also am noticing, as I walk around the tree, that one side of the tree has this interesting moss, but the other side doesn't have any moss. As I'm observing, I feel my brain filling up with deep-thinking questions. Does anyone have any questions they would like to share?

(pause and allow students to share)

My questions were like some of yours: I'm wondering how the bark gets all those deep crevasses. I'm wondering if this ant has a home somewhere in the tree and if there are any other ants nearby. I'm wondering why the moss is only growing on one side of the tree. I'm wondering how old this tree is. I'm wondering what kind of tree this is. Wow, so many questions coming from just a little bit of observing. That's what scientists do! Now we might not have the answers to our questions right now, but they are certainly getting my brain thinking.

- Invite students to wander with a partner to find a nature spot to sit or stand in. Emphasize the importance of starting with careful observation. (Students might wish to draw and label some of the things they observe.) Encourage them to use their senses (except possibly taste!) when they observe.

- Allow time for students to complete the observations and diagram on the Wonder Walk template outside. Depending on time, questions can be added when you have returned to class.
- Invite students to share their Wonder Walk observations and questions with a partner, or have a few students share with the class.

WONDER WALK EXTENSION

Recently, I discovered an amazing picture book called *What's in Your Pocket?: Collecting Nature Treasures* by Heather L. Montgomery. In it, we meet nine real-life scientists who, as kids, explored the great outdoors and collected treasures: seedpods, fossils, worms, and more. Observing, sorting, and classifying their treasures taught them scientific skills, and sometimes led to ground-breaking discoveries. As an extension to taking your students on a Wonder Walk, or possibly on a follow-up walk, you can use this book prior to your walk and invite students to find one object from nature (stone, leaf, blade of grass, pinecone, etc.) to bring back. Students use the My Wonder Walk template on page 98 to record their observations and questions about their object.

Lesson: Introducing the Scientific Method

The scientific method is a valuable tool used to solve scientific problems in a logical way, and is an important first step in conducting class science experiments. This lesson, as a follow-up to your Wonder Walk, helps bring more meaning to the scientific method, as students are able to connect the process to their own observations and questions.

- Remind students that they were taking on the role of a scientist on their Wonder Walk. Scientists observe, study closely, and ask questions to try to learn things about the world. Explain that these are the first steps in what's called the *scientific method*. Real scientists use the scientific method to study, learn, and try to come up with answers.
- Explain that, after observing and asking questions, a scientist focuses on one of their questions and makes a prediction about it. In science, a prediction is called a *hypothesis*.

    For example, on my Wonder Walk, I noticed moss growing on one side of the tree and I wondered about that. I have been thinking a lot about that moss, and my hypothesis is that I think it has something to do with the sunlight. Maybe one side of the tree gets more sun, so it's dryer—maybe moss can't grow when it's too hot.

- Explain that if you were a real scientist trying to figure out why moss only grows on one side of a tree, you would need to come up with some way to test that by conducting an experiment.
- Explain and record the steps of the scientific method on the whiteboard or chart stand:

    1. Make observations
    2. Come up with an interesting question based on the observations
    3. Develop a hypothesis or prediction to go along with the question
    4. Experiment and test
    5. Gather and record results of the tests and draw conclusions

6. Compare results with your hypothesis
7. Share and discuss results

Tell students that a simple way of thinking about the scientific method is this:

What do you think will happen? (hypothesis)
What is happening? (observations)
What happened compared to what you thought would happen? (conclusion)

Looking for more ideas on science experiments using the Scientific Method? Check out the Little Bins, Big Hands website: https://littlebinsforlittlehands.com/using-scientific-method-experiments-kids/

- Explain to students that, during their Wonder Walk activity, they had already started their own scientific method! They had observed and wondered—the first two steps.
- Invite students to choose one of their Wonder Walk questions and to try to make a prediction or hypothesis. Depending on grade level, your students could continue to develop and/or conduct their own experiment, or this lesson can be used to launch into class experiments.
- Reflect on the lesson. Remind students that scientists are deep thinkers who ask deep questions about the world around them, and that sometimes these questions lead to important discoveries.

SCIENTIFIC METHOD ANCHOR BOOKS

There is no better way to help students understand and get excited about the scientific method than by sharing engaging picture books with memorable characters engaged in the scientific process!

RECOMMENDED BOOKS ON THE SCIENTIFIC METHOD

Charlotte the Scientist Finds a Cure by Camille Andros
Charlotte the Scientist Is Squished by Camille Andros
Ada Twist – Scientist by Andrea Beaty
Cece Loves Science by Kimberly Derting
What Is Science? by Rebecca Kai Dotlich
My Dog is Not a Scientist by Betsy Ellor
The Princess and the Petri Dish by Sue Fliess
Mary Had a Little Lab by Sue Fliess

My Brother the Duck by Pat Zietlow Miller
11 Experiments That Failed by Jenny Offill
Darwin's Super-Pooping Worm Spectacular by Polly Owe
The Great Stink: How Joseph Bazalgette Solved London's Poop Pollution Problem by Colleen Paeff
Mesmerized: How Ben Franklin Solved a Mystery that Baffled All of France by Mara Rockliff
The Mystery of the Monarchs by Barb Rosenstock

My Wonder Walk

Name: _____

My Observations	My Wonderings
I see…	I'm wondering…
_____	_____
_____	_____
_____	_____
_____	_____
_____	_____
_____	_____

My question: _____

My hypothesis (prediction): _____

_____

Scientist Biographies

Sharing picture-book biographies about real-life scientists is a simple way to link literacy and thinking to your science program. There are many amazing books celebrating the life work of a huge selection of scientists in all different fields—astronomers, botanists, chemists, and more. They are true stories of passion, courage, determination, and perseverance, and will inspire both you and your students as you learn about true scientific heroes. These books are rich with information and are perfect read-alouds for inviting connections, questions, inferences, and transformed thinking. These books will also help to introduce different scientific fields and reinforce the scientific process.

Depending on grade level and the time you wish you spend, you could either choose one or two books connected to your science unit to share, or dive a little deeper into the world of scientists to inspire a inquiry unit on the impact of science on our world. Use the Ground-Breaking Scientist templates on page 101 (Intermediate) or 102 (Primary), or the A Sensational Scientist template on page 103.

Astronomers
Mae Among the Stars by Roda Ahmed
What Miss Mitchell Saw by Hayley Barrett
Always Looking Up: Nancy Grace Roman, Astronomer by Laura Gehl
Caroline's Comets: A True Story by Emily Arnold McCully
Starry Messenger: Galileo Galilei by Peter Sís
Classified: The Secret Career of Mary Golda Ross, Cherokee Aerospace Engineer by Traci Sorell

Chemists
Mario and the Hole in the Sky: How a Chemist Saved Our Planet by Elizabeth Rusch
Marie Curie (Little People, Big Dreams) by Maria Isabel Sanchez Vegara

Computing Scientists
Ada Byron Lovelace and the Thinking Machine by Laurie Wallmark
Grace Hopper: Queen of Computer Code by Laurie Wallmark

Entomologists
Summer Birds: The Butterflies of Maria Merian by Margarita Engle
Evelyn the Adventurous Entomologist: The True Story of a World-Traveling Bug Hunter by Christine Evans
Small Wonders: Jean-Henri Fabre and His World of Insects by Matthew Clark Smith

Environmentalists
Spring After Spring: How Rachel Carson Inspired the Environmental Movement by Stephanie Roth Sisson
Note: Jane Goodall books would also fit here

Inventors
Just Like Rube Goldberg: The Incredible True Story of the Man Behind the Machines by Sarah Aronson
Timeless Thomas: How Thomas Edison Changed Our Lives by Gene Barretta
Whoosh! Lonnie Johnson's Super-Soaking Stream of Inventions by Chris Barton
Josephine and Her Dishwashing Machine: Josephine Cochrane's Bright Invention Makes a Splash by Kate Hannigan

Marine Biologists
Manfish: A Story of Jacques Cousteau by Jennifer Berne
Secrets of the Sea: The Story of Jeanne Power, Revolutionary Marine Scientist by Evan Griffith
Shark Lady: The True Story of How Eugenie Clark Became the Ocean's Most Fearless Scientist by Jess Keating
The Fantastic Undersea Life of Jacques Cousteau by Dan Yaccarino

Mathematicians
Nothing Stopped Sophie: The Story of Unshakable Mathematician Sophie Germain by Cheryl Bardoe
Counting on Katherine: How Katherine Johnson Saved Apollo 13 by Helaine Becker

The Girl With a Mind For Math: The Story of Raye Montague by Julia Finley Mosca

Margaret and the Moon by Dean Robbins

Hidden Figures: The True Story of Four Black Women and the Space Race by Margot Lee Shetterly

Microbiologists

All in a Drop: How Antony van Leeuwenhoek Discovered an Invisible World by Lori Alexander

Never Give Up: Dr. Kati Karikó and the Race for the Future of Vaccines by Debbie Dadey

Naturalists

The Leaf Detective: How Margaret Lowman Uncovered Secrets in the Rainforest by Heather Lang

The Girl Who Drew Butterflies: How Maria Merian's Art Changed Science by Joyce Sidman

Oceanographers

Solving the Puzzle Under the Sea: Marie Tharp Maps the Ocean Floor by Robert Burleigh

Paleontologists

When Sue Found Sue: Sue Hendrickson Discovers Her T. Rex by Toni Buzzeo

Barnum's Bones by Tracey Fern

Dinosaur Lady: The Daring Discoveries of Mary Anning, the First Paleontologist by Linda Skeers

Physicists

On a Beam of Light by Jennifer Byrne

Queen of Physics: How Wu Chien Shiung Helped Unlock the Secrets of the Atom by Teresa Robeson

Zoologists

Anne and Her Tower of Giraffes: The Adventurous Life of the First Giraffologist by Karling Gray

Me…: Jane Goodall's Life with the Chimps by Jeanette Winter

Ground-Breaking Scientist 1

My Name: _____

Title: _____ Author: _____

Name of the Scientist

_____

Date of Birth _____

Date of Death (if applicable): _____

Childhood

_____

_____

_____

Field of Science

_____

Famous for

_____

_____

_____

Impact or Influence on the World

_____

_____

_____

Interesting Facts

_____

_____

_____

Ground-Breaking Scientist 2

Name: _____

Scientist's Name: _____

Born: _____

Died: _____

Famous for _____

_____

_____

_____

Interesting Facts _____

_____

_____

_____

A Sensational Scientist

My Name: _____

Name of the Scientist: _____

Date of Birth: _____

Date of Death (if applicable): _____

Famous for:

_____

_____

A little background about	My thoughts about
_____	_____

7 Thinking in Social Studies

Back in the day (here I go again!), Social Studies was primarily taught with the use of textbooks, which were often written like encyclopedias, overwhelming with factual information, but with little to no consideration of student interest or reading level. Thankfully, over the past 10 to 15 years, there has been a significant rise in the amount, quality, and variety of interesting children's literature available to use in a Social Studies classroom, inspiring more teachers to integrate them into their units.

Besides literacy, Social Studies has always been my favorite subject to teach. I love how easily literacy and Social Studies content can be connected, and how many opportunities there are to nudge students beyond the literal facts into a place of deeper thinking. Whenever I began planning my Social Studies units, you could always find me in the library, searching out stories to weave into my lessons. Using picture books in Social Studies helped me introduce new topics and provided an entry point to complex or challenging issues. Whether the content was cultural diversity, natural resources, immigration, community, explorers, government, or first contact, I always had a stack of picture-book teaching partners on hand to help me link thinking with my Social Studies curriculum.

In this chapter I provide three examples of Social Studies units where picture books are used to teach content and nudge thinking. Along with the read-alouds, students engage in both oral discussions and written responses.

Reading and Thinking Across Canada

After years of launching my Canada unit with a very large blank map of Canada and an oh-so-lengthy list of things my students needed to include on their map (don't forget to color each province and shade the oceans, thank you), and followed by literal (yet colorful!) Provincial travel brochures, I realized I needed to stretch my own teaching in order to stretch my students' thinking! Reading and Thinking Across Canada looks at the history of Canada through historical events from each province. Each lesson begins with a read-aloud that focuses on the province, event, and time period. Thinking strategies are modeled during the read-aloud, and students are engaged in partner and/or class discussions before, during, and after the story. A response sheet is provided for students to record information about the event and their thinking about it.

To be fair, there is nothing wrong with provincial travel brochures. But if our goal is to engage students in moving beyond literal facts and to help build knowledge, the brochures don't quite cut it anymore. My students loved learning about the history of Canada through these knowledge-rich read-alouds and were buzzing about their learning. They were engaged—they learned, made connections, and asked questions, some even shed a few tears, and many would erupt in applause when the last sentence was read.

Introductory Lesson: One Word

- Write the word *Canada* on a chart paper. Invite students to look at the word and think about the word. While they are thinking about the word *Canada*, ask them to

  1. make a connection
  2. create a visual image
  3. find a feeling

- Invite students to think for a minute, then share their ideas with a partner. Bring the class together and invite students to share their ideas. Record the ideas on the board around the word *Canada*, creating a web.
- Write the word *History* on the board and invite students to share what they think the word means. Ask them to find a smaller word inside the word that may help them (a hint: *his, or, is, hi* won't help!). Circle the word *story*. Explain that history is really the story of an event, a place, or a person from the past. Tell the students that you noticed that the word *history* was not included on the One Word *Canada* web. Ask students why they think that is (*Most were thinking of Canada now, not in the past*). Explain that learning about the past helps us better understand the present.
- Tell students that for the next few weeks (or months), you will be learning about the stories of Canada's past by reading stories about true events, places, and people from each of the provinces. Tell students that the stories, you hope, will help stretch their thinking about Canada. Explain that after you have finished, you will be coming back to the One Word web and adding their new thinking to it.
- Post the Canada One Word web in the classroom so that you can add to it as needed throughout the unit.
- Pass out a map of Canada (already labeled!) for students to color as they travel across the country with stories.

Reading and Thinking Across Canada Weekly Lessons

These lessons can be taught either in geographical order, starting in BC and working east across the country, or in chronological order, if you prefer to introduce the stories in sequence of events and include a timeline. As with any story you share with your class, it's important to read them yourself before sharing them. Most of these stories also include back notes, which will help provide you with the factual information the story is depicting.

- Begin each lesson by locating the province from which the story takes place. Use a map of Canada to locate the province. Students can color the province on their own maps. If you have access to an "old school" map of Canada, you can post small photocopies of the book covers on each province as you read them (see sample on page 106).

Grade 4 sample using the template on page 110

Reading and Thinking Across Canada

- Write the title of the story on the whiteboard or chart stand. Show the students the cover of the book. Ask them what they might be wondering about the story.
- Remind students that the book is based on a true story in Canada's history. Because many students might not have background knowledge about the event you will be sharing, you can use the back notes to provide students with a Book Bite (see page 67), which could include key dates, background information, and any new vocabulary they might need prior to listening to the story. Post a list of key vocabulary connected to the story and/or event on the whiteboard or chart stand under the title and province, and review the vocabulary words with students.
- As you read the story aloud, pause, model your thinking (connections, questions, etc.), and invite students to participate in the read-aloud/think aloud process.
- After the story is complete, spend a few minutes summarizing the story, the facts learned from the story, and their thinking about the story.

Story summary	Facts we learned	Thoughts we have

For those who notice students struggling with either not enough or far too much detail in their story summary, try the Somebody–Wanted–But–So–Then strategy (see page 84). It's a game changer!

- Pass out the Reading and Thinking Across Canada response template on page 110 for students to complete independently (see sample on page 106).

Reading and Thinking Across Canada

Name: Emma and the Silk train

Province: BC   Title: Robin ↑   Author: Julie Lawson

Story Summary	Facts I Learned	Thoughts I have
This girl called Emma gets lost when she is looking for silk that is floating around the farm after the silk train crashes.	• Silk train carried silk from China across the CP rail acros Canada in 1930s. • Silk trains went very fast and if they were slow you didn't get paid.	I didn't know about the silk trains. I like that they went so fast and you had to move over for them. I am surprised only 1 silk train ever crashed.

READING AND THINKING ACROSS CANADA BOOK LIST

These picture books are based on true events from Canadian history and are listed in geographical order, beginning in the west, working east, and ending up in the Far North. I have included a brief summary and done my best to provide approximate dates for each book, in case you prefer to work chronologically and/ or develop a timeline. Most of the books include back notes, which are helpful for providing background knowledge to you and your students. While I have included several titles for some provinces, due to the time you will need to complete the unit, I recommend sharing only one book per province.

British Columbia

When Emily Carr Met Woo by Monica Kullin (early 1900s)

The Jade Necklace by Paul Yee (Chinese immigration to Canada, 1900s)

Emma and the Silk Train by Julie Lawson (silk train derailment, CP rail, Asian imports, 1927)

Secret of the Dance by Andrea Spalding (banning of the potlatch in Haida Gwaii, 1935)

Mr. Hiroshi's Garden by Maxine Trottier (Japanese Internment, WW11, 1942)

One Million Trees: a True Story by Kristen Balouch (family joins tree reforestation project, 1979)

Alberta

Josepha: A Prairie Boy's Story by Jim McGugan (European immigration to North America, early 1900s)

Flip Flop Flapjack: Wildhorse Jack and the First Stampede Breakfast by Brenda Joyce Leahy (Calgary Stampede pancake tradition, 1923)

Saving Thunder the Great by Leanne Shirtcliff (Fort McMurray Fire, 2016)

Saskatchewan

Honouring the Buffalo: A Plains Cree Legend by Ray Lavallee

Li'l Shadd: A Story of Ujima by Miriam Korner (Dr. Alfred Shadd, first African-Canadian pioneer and his relationship with Indigenous community, 1890)

If These Places Could Talk: Snapshots of Saskatchewan by Crista Bradley (places in Saskatchewan tell their stories in first person)

Manitoba

Finding Winnie: The True Story of the World's Most Famous Bear by Lindsay Mattick (true story of the bear who inspired Winnie the Pooh during WW1, 1914)

Ontario

The Red Sash by Jean E. Pendziwo (young Metis boy who lives near the fur trading post near Lake Superior, 1700s)

The Log Driver's Waltz by Wade Hemsworth (based on the song that celebrates the profession of log driving, 1800s)

Laura Secord: A Story of Courage by Janet Lunn (Laura Secord's heroism during the War of 1812)

Out of the Woods: A True Story of an Unforgettable Event by Rebecca Bond (fire breaks out in small boarding house in logging community near Lake Ontario, 1914)

Go Home Bay by Susan Vande Griek (Group of Seven artist Tom Thompson teaches a young girl to paint one summer, early 20th century)

I Am Not a Number by Jenny Kay Dupuis (experiences in a Residential School, 1928)

The Secret Path by Gordon Downie (story of 12-year-old Chanie Wenjack, who died trying to walk home from Residential school in Northern Ontario, 1966)

Quebec

The Sugaring Off Party by Jonathon London (grandmother details a traditional maple sugar party to her grandson, early 1900s)

Just Like New by Ainslie Manson (Quebecois children send gently used toys to children in England during WWII, 1940)

The Hockey Sweater by Roch Carrier (author's true story of being ridiculed and taken off the bench for wearing a rival Toronto Maple Leafs sweater to a hockey practice, 1945)

Nova Scotia

Africville by Shauntay Grant (amazing and shameful history of Black refugee community living in Halifax, 1840s)

Explosion Newsie by Jacqueline Halsey (explosion of two war ships in Halifax Harbour, child labour, 1917)

Viola Desmond Won't Be Budged by Jody Warner (women started civil rights movement after being jailed for sitting in the wrong seat in a movie theater, 1946)

Free As the Wind: Saving the Wild Horses on Sable Island by Joseph Bastille (young student writes letter to Prime Minister asking to stop the slaughter of horses, 1960)

Boy of the Deeps by Ian Wallace (life experiences of Canadian coal miners, 1960s)

New Brunswick

The River Fiddles by Ron Caldwell (origins of NB's legendary Fiddlers on the Tobique Festival)

F Is for Fiddlehead: A New Brunswick Alphabet by Marilyn Lohnes (New Brunswick facts, traditions, history, and famous people)

What-cha Doing by Kim Renton (maple sugaring)

Newfoundland and Labrador

Heroes of Isle aux Morts by Alice Walsh (true story of the wreck of the Despatch, 1872)

Duncan's Way by Ian Wallace (life of an Atlantic-coast fishing family, 1980s)

Dolphin SOS by Roy Miki (true story of the teens rescuing dolphins who are stuck under the ice, 2009)

PEI

Encounter by Brittany Luby (explorer Jacques Cartier's first expedition to North America and his encounter with Indigenous fisherman, 1534)

The Summer of Marco Polo by Bettye Stroude (famous clipper ship runs aground off the coast of PEI, near Lucy Maude's house, 1883)

Lucy Maude Montgomery: The Author of Anne of Green Gables by Alexandra Wallner (the early life of the famous author, who lived 1874–1942)

Yukon

Northern Lights: The Soccer Trails by Michael Arvaarluk Kusugak (legend of the Northern Lights, told by an Inuit grandmother to her granddaughter)

Klondike Cat by Julie Lawson (Noah and his father travel to the Klondike to join the Gold Rush, 1896)

Northwest Territories

Lands and Cultures of Canada's Northwest Territories The Land Is Our Storybook series (Strong Nations Publishing) (six books, each celebrating the seasons, communities, and celebrations of a different Indigenous group)

Nunavut

Alego by Ningeokuluk Teevee (curious Inuit girl encounters fascinating sea creatures while collecting clams with her grandmother, late 1900s)

Una Huna? What Is This? by Susan Aglukark (a young girl experiences both excitement and doubt when traders come to her land, 1920s)

Kisimi Taimaippaktut Angirrarijarani/Only in My Hometown by Angnakuluk Friesen (life in a small Inuit community)

Unipkaaqtuat Arvianit by Mark Kalluak (author shares favorite stories passed down from his community and his family)

Lesson: Concluding the Unit

One student's comment, when reflecting on some of the transformed thinking experienced during the Reading and Thinking Across Canada unit: "Well, Canada is actually not as friendly as I thought it was! But the good thing is that some of those bad things happened in the past so it's good to know that we learned from our mistakes and are trying to be more friendly now."

- After reading and thinking across Canada, repost the Canada word web you created before you began the unit.
- Ask students to look over the words they had included.

  Now that we have learned more about the history of Canada, how has our thinking stretched? What new words could we add to our web? Think for 1, talk for 2, and share for 3.

- Use a different color to add a second layer to the word web around the initial one. Reflect on the fact that the original ideas about Canada didn't disappear but that the class's thinking has certainly stretched.

One Word activity, Grade 5 class. The outer notes are written in different colors from the first notes in the middle, making the stretched thinking more noticeable.

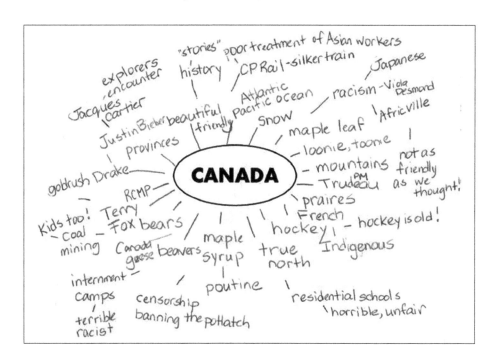

Reading and Thinking Across Canada

Name: _____

Province: _____ Title: _____ Author: _____

Story Summary	Facts I Learned	Thoughts I have
_____	_____	_____
_____	_____	_____
_____	_____	_____
_____	_____	_____
_____	_____	_____
_____	_____	_____
_____	_____	_____
_____	_____	_____

Story Scene that Sticks!

Pembroke Publishers ©2024 *Powerful Thinking* by Adrienne Gear ISBN 9781551383637

Thinking About Global Justice

Whether we teach elementary children or older students, they all can benefit from global education. All learners, even our youngest, can begin to develop empathy for people who look different, are treated as different, or live under different conditions. We can introduce our students to basic geography and history, and help build their awareness of the complex global issues and inequitable treatment facing many people around the world. And for this, as with any unit I teach, I turn to picture books to guide and support my lessons. Picture books depicting real-life global justice issues help students access complex, sometimes challenging, issues in a manageable way. The read-aloud strategy helps students build knowledge and supports their critical thinking by promoting discussions and questions around global issues.

GLOBAL JUSTICE ANCHOR BOOKS

I believe these picture books best depict a wide range of global justice issues. Depending on your grade level, specific curriculum content, and time set aside for this unit, you can select the issues and books you wish to focus on. Alternatively, you may wish to dive deeper into a specific issue using a targeted text set of anchor books.

Assimilation
Shi-Shi-Etko by Nicola Campbell
I Am Not a Number by Jenny K. Dupuis
Stolen Words by Melanie Florence
When I Was Eight by Christy Jordan-Fenton
When We Were Alone by David Alexander Robertson
The Orange Shirt Story: The True Story of Orange Shirt Day by Phyllis Webstad
Phyllis's Orange Shirt by Phyllis Webstad

Censorship
This Book Is Banned by Raj Haldar
The Great Banned-Books Bake Sale by Aya Khali
The Stamp Collector by Jennifer Lanthier
Secret of the Dance by Andrea Spalding

Civil Rights/ Racism
Something Happened In Our Town: A Child's Story about Racial Injustice by Marianne Celano
The Story of Ruby Bridges by Robert Coles
We March by Shane Evans
Rosa by Nikki Giovanni
We All Belong: A Children's Book About Diversity, Race and Empathy by Nathalie Goss
I Have a Dream by Dr. Martin Luther King Jr
Let's Talk About Race by Julius Lester
Nelson Mandela by Kadir Nelson
The Stone Thrower by Jael Ealey Richardson
Viola Desmond Won't Be Budged by Jody Nyasha Warner

Colonization/First Contact
Encounter by Brittany Luby
The Rabbits by John Marsden
The Red Sash by Jean E. Pendziwol
Encounter by Jane Yolen

Dictatorship
Sparrow Girl by Sarah Pennypacker
This Is a Dictatorship by Equipol Plantel
Isang Harding Papel by Augie Rivera
The Composition by Antonio Skarameta

Emancipation
Underground: Finding the Light to Freedom by Shane Evans
The Birdman: A Journey with the Underground Railroad's Most Daring Abolitionist by Troon Harrison
Henry's Freedom Box: A True Story from the Underground Railroad by Ellen Levine
If You Traveled on the Underground Railroad by Ellen Levine
The Patchwork Path: A Quilt Map to Freedom by Betty Stroud

Exploitation
I Like, I Don't Like by Anna Baccelliere
Brave Girl: Clara and the Shirtwaist Makers' Strike of 1909 by Michelle Markel

Malala, a Brave Girl from Pakistan/Iqbal, a Brave Boy from Pakistan: Two Stories of Bravery by Jeanette Winter

Homelessness and Poverty
Those Shoes by Maribeth Bolts
Maddi's Fridge by Lois Brandt
Yard Sale by Eve Bunting
Home by Tonya Lippert
Saturday at the Food Pantry by Diane O'Neill
Shelter: Homelessness in our Community by Lois Petterson
Lunch Every Day by Kathryn Otoshi
On Our Street: Our First Talk About Poverty by Dr. Jillian Roberts
I Don't Have Enough: A First Look at Poverty by Pat Thomas
The Can Man by Laura Williams

Immigration
Gleam and Glow by Eve Bunting
One Green Apple by Eve Bunting
Saving the Butterfly by Helen Cooper
Mama's Nightingale: A Story of Immigration and Separation by Edwidge Danticat
The Day the War Came by Nicola Davies
My Beautiful Birds by Suzanna Del Rizzo
My Two Blankets by Irena Kobold
Lost and Found Cat: The True Story of Kunkush's Incredible Journey by Doug Kuntz
To the Other Side by Erika Meza
My Name Is Not Refugee by Kate Milner
The Banana Leaf Ball by Katie Smith Milway
Watch Me: A Story of Immigration and Inspiration by Doyin Richards

Stepping Stones: A Refugee Family's Journey by Margriet Ruurs
The Journey by Francesca Sanna
Grandfather's Journey by Allen Say
Adrift at Sea: A Vietnamese Boy's Story of Survival by Marsha Forchuk Skrypuch
Angel Child, Dragon Child by Michele Maria Surat
Migrant by Maxine Trottier
Wishes by Muon Thi Van
Four Feet, Two Sandals by Karen Lynn Williams

Persecution
Rose Blanche by Christophe Gallaz (Holocaust)
The Harmonica by Tony Johnston (Holocaust)
Naomi's Tree by Joy Kogawa (Japanese Internment)
Baseball Saved Us by Ken Mochizuki (Japanese Internment)
Love in the Library by Maggie Tokuda-Hall (Japanese Internment)
Stone Angel by Jane Yolen (Holocaust)

Segregation/Racism
White Socks Only by Evelyn Coleman
The Story of Ruby Bridges by Robert Coles
Africville by Shauntay Grant
Antiracist Baby by Ibram X. Kendi
Let's Talk About Race by Julius Lester
Our Skin: A First Conversation About Race by Megan Madison
The Stone Thrower by Jael Ealey Richardson
On the Playground: Our First Talk About Prejudice by Jillian Roberts
Separate Is Never Equal by Duncan Tonatium
Freedom Summer by Deborah Wiles

Lesson: Global Justice

- Write the term *Global Justice* on the whiteboard or chart. Tell students you are starting a new unit called Global Justice. Ask them what they think that term means. Invite them to share their ideas with a partner.
- Explain that *global justice* is a term for the idea that everybody around the world is treated equally and fairly. Ask students if they think that there is global justice everywhere in the world. If they don't think so, invite them to share examples of how people are not treated equally (*racism, bullying, poverty*, etc.).
- Explain that the term *global justice* is a big umbrella term under which there are many different global issues. Pass out the Issues in Global Justice template on page 115. Explain that the global justice issues they will be learning about are listed on the page.
- Invite students to work with a partner to record what they know or think they know about each issue. They can add connections, examples, events, people's

names. Tell the students that likely they will have heard of some of the words, but not all of them. Remind them that this is not a test—they are to record their thoughts and not to worry about being right.

Unit Lessons

- Focus each lesson on one global justice issue and select an anchor book from the list (or one you know) depicting a true event representative of the issue.
- Begin each lesson by introducing the global justice issue using the One Word activity (see page 66). Write the word on the board and invite students to share what they know or think they know about the topic and any connections they might have.
- Before reading, provide some basic background knowledge about the issue or topic for them: dates, names, locations, and a short explanation of the issue—without giving away too much. This background information is often located in the back notes of the book.
- While you read, model your thinking by pausing and sharing your questions, connections, feelings, inferences, etc. with students. Invite students to share their thinking as well.
- After the read-aloud is complete, invite students to find a partner and share one thought they have about the story. Use this Partner Sharing chart.

Depending on grade level, you might choose one of the fictional stories depicting the event as an access point for the topic.

Visual comprehension is helpful for some students who find it challenging to sit for long periods of time. Offer students visualizing sheets for anyone who would like to draw while they listen. Encourage them to record visual images that are connected to the story rather than random doodling.

Partner Sharing

> **Share your thinking!**
> Tell your partner…
> - a connection you made to the story
> - a new fact you learned from the story
> - a question you have about the story
> - something in the story that surprised or shocked you
> - a feeling you have after reading the story
> - why you think the author wrote this story

I don't assign independent written responses after each lesson, but you could occasionally opt to have students record their thoughts after a read-aloud and class discussion, if time permits. They can use the Exploring Global Justice template on page 116.

- Create a three-part chart on the whiteboard or screen with the headings *Story Summary, Facts I Learned, Thoughts I Have*. Starting on the left and working across, invite students to participate and record their ideas on the chart.
- As you work through the weekly global issues, draw students' attention to the connections between them. While the global issues are different, they share some common themes.

REFLECTION

After completing your selection of global issue read-alouds, culminate the unit with some reflection, discussion, and stretched thinking.

- If you started the unit with the One Word activity, revisit the anchor chart and web you created. Invite students to stretch their thinking about global justice and share some new thoughts they have. Using a different-colored marker, create an outer web and record their new ideas. Reflect on the fact that, by learning about the different types of global justice or injustice, they added knowledge and deepened their thinking about these important issues.
- Discuss the fact that, while all the issues they learned about were different, they were all considered issues of global justice. Ask them what they think connected the issues, and what the issues have in common. Share the Devel-

oping a Powerful Understanding of Global Justice template on page 117 and invite students to respond (see sample, below).

Grade 7 sample: reflection on racial issues after hearing the story "White Socks Only" by Evelyn Coleman (See lesson on Reflection on pages 113–114)

Reflection .... (What this story makes me think about:.. How this story connects to **global justice**)

Global justice. Racial Segregation existed. It's not okay. The colour of your skin shouldn't matter. African people are not less that Caucasian people. All peoples should have equal rights. Our world is full of colour. We must all be well-educated on the issues of the past, and in the present. Our colourful, multicultural world is special. Bathrooms and restaurants should be colourful! It's more beautiful that way. Having a blank white paper is boring. Imagine a bright colourful piece of paper! Racial segregation is NOT OKAY! I'm glad it doesn't happen anymore. Racial Segregation is not okay...

LESSON EXTENSION

Invite students to choose one global justice story that they felt strongly about. Ask them to create either a diary entry or a letter, in first person, in the voice of the main character. Remind them to include relevant information about the character's background, experience, home, family, and the events outlined in the story. Tell them their letter or diary entry should include

- an introduction
- your personal background (where and when you were born, family, etc.)
- your experiences
- details about the events from the story
- your feelings and reaction to what is happening around you
- your hopes for the future

Issues in Global Justice

Name: _____

What do you know about these issues?

Colonization

_____

_____

Emancipation

_____

_____

Segregation

_____

_____

Racism

_____

_____

Civil Rights

_____

_____

Assimilation

_____

_____

Dictatorship

_____

_____

Censorship

_____

_____

Persecution

_____

_____

Pembroke Publishers ©2024 *Powerful Thinking* by Adrienne Gear ISBN 9781551383637

Exploring Global Justice

Name: _____

Global Issue: _____

Title: _____   Author: _____

Main Character: _____   Location and date of event (if known): _____

Story Summary
_____
_____
_____
_____

Facts I Learned
_____
_____
_____
_____

Thoughts I Have (connections, feelings, reactions, questions)
_____
_____
_____
_____

Pembroke Publishers ©2024 *Powerful Thinking* by Adrienne Gear ISBN 9781551383637

Developing a Powerful Understanding of Global Justice

After reading and learning about the many different examples of global justice issues, what are you thinking about? What do all the different global issues have in common? What is the motivation behind these issues? Why is there injustice in the world?

_____

_____

_____

_____

_____

_____

_____

_____

_____

_____

_____

_____

_____

_____

_____

Pembroke Publishers ©2024 *Powerful Thinking* by Adrienne Gear ISBN 9781551383637

Exploring Community

Community is a unit of study often explored in early primary grades. Beyond learning about the characteristics of a local community, even young students can begin to think about their role and responsibility as community members. This lesson, adapted from one of my lessons in *Powerful Understanding*, looks at ways students can begin to see themselves as active community members.

COMMUNITY ANCHOR BOOKS

These books introduce the concept of local community and the people and places within a community.

Which Communities Do You Belong To? A Children's Picture Book About Community, Citizenship, Family, and Neighborhood by Julien Bodrieu
My Neighborhood: Places and Faces by Lisa Bullard
On the Town: A Community Adventure by Judith Caseley
National Geographic Kids Readers: Helpers in Your Neighborhood by Shira Evans
Exploring Our World: Neighborhoods and Communities by Kathleen M. Hollenbeck

Walking in the City With Jane: A Story of Jane Jacobs by Susan Hughes
Community Helpers Then and Now by Bobbie Kalman
Helpers in my Community by Bobbie Kalman
Places in my Community by Bobbie Kalman
Who Is My Neighbor? by Amy-Jill Levine
A Park Connects Us by Sarah Nelson
Whose Hands Are These? A Community Helper Guessing Game by Miranda Paul

Lesson: Our Local Community

The first part of this unit invites students to explore the characteristics of their local community—people, places, and activities.

- Write the word *Community* on the whiteboard or chart stand. Tell students you are going to be exploring this topic over the next few weeks.
- Invite students to Think for 1, Talk for 2, and Share for 3 (see page 24) about community. Alternatively, you could use the One Word activity (see page 66) to stimulate a discussion. Use these questions to help guide students' thinking:

  - What is a community?
  - What are some places in your local community?
  - What are some activities you participate in your community?
  - Who are people you might find in your community? What roles do they play?
  - Why is community important?

- Brainstorm different places in your local community (*school, library, community centre, stores, restaurants, parks,* etc.). Ask why these places are important in the community (*They are gathering places for people in the community*). Invite students to share what their favorite place in their community is and why.
- Brainstorm different people in the community (*teachers, police officers, librarians, nurses, doctors, dentists, shop keepers, postal workers,* etc.). Ask why these people are important in the community (*They help others*).
- Read one of the community anchor books. Copy and pass out the My Community and Me template on page 122. Invite students to draw, label, and color places and people in their community. Encourage students to label using proper names if they know them; "Instead of writing *library*, write *Hillcrest Library*."

Lesson: Being a Community Member

In this lesson, you will be exploring what it means to be an active, responsible, and caring community member.

These books illustrate ways to be active, caring, and responsible community members. Many feature people who notice a problem in their community and actively work to resolve and make a difference.

Rise Up and Write It: With Real Mail, Posters, and More! by Nandini Ahuja

Can We Help? Kids Volunteering to Help Their Communities by George Ancona

I Can Do It Too! by Karen Baicker

Maybe Something Beautiful: How Art Transformed a Neighborhood by F. Isabel Campoy

Follow the Moon Home: A Tale of One Idea, Twenty Kids, and a Hundred Sea Turtles by Philippe Cousteau

What Can a Citizen Do? by Dave Eggers

Community Soup by Alma Fullerton

You, Me, We: A Celebration of Peace and Community by Arun Gandhi

Maybe I Can Love My Neighbor Too? by Jennifer Grant

Kamala and Maya's Big Idea by Meena Harris

Pond by Jim LaMarche

Green Green: Community Gardening Story by Marie Lamba

We Live Here Too!: Kids Talk About Good Citizenship by Nancy Loewen

Counting on Community by Innosanto Nagara

The Big Beach Cleanup by Charlotte Offsay

Look Where We Live!: A First Book of Community Building by Scot Ritchie

Just Help! How to Build a Better World by Sonia Sotomayor

We're Better Together: A Book About Community by Eileen Spinelli

Every Dog in the Neighborhood by Philip Christian Stead

Black Beach: A Community, an Oil Spill, and the Origin of Earth Day by John and Shaunna Stith

Our Little Kitchen by Jillian Tamaki

Hey, Wall: A Story of Art and Community by Susan Verde

Our World Is a Family: Our Community Can Change the World by Miry Whitehill and Jennifer Jackson

Dear Street by Lindsay Zier-Vogal

- Remind students that they have been exploring what a community is, and the people, places, and activities connected to their local community.

   Yesterday, we explored different people in our local community. Today, we are going to expand our thinking a little and explore how our community helps us and what we might do to help our community.

- Ask students to think about ways the community makes our lives better. How does our community help us? (*places to learn: school, library; places to play, swim, skate: parks and community centres; places to shop and eat: stores and restaurants; hospitals and doctors help us stay healthy; police officers keep us safe; farmers' markets; libraries for borrowing books; etc.*)
- Brainstorm and record ideas on the left side of a two-column chart.
- After listing everything a community provides us, ask students what it makes them think about. Invite students to share their new thinking about communities.

   Before, when I thought about my community, I would just think about the people and places in it. But now I'm really thinking just how much our local community helps us and provides things for us. It doesn't seem right anymore that I should benefit from all the support in my community but not do anything to give back.

- Read one (or more) of the anchor books (see recommended list on page 119). Discuss ways in which the person or people in the story helped or supported their community.
- Ask students, *What could we do, as a class, to help support or show our gratitude to our local community*? Brainstorm ideas and record them on the right side of the chart table.

How our community helps us	How we can help our community
Schools to learn in Parks to play in Hospitals and dentists Community centres to swim, skate, and meet friends Farmers' markets Police to keep us safe Restaurants and shops	Picking up garbage in the park and schoolyard Shopping locally at farmers' markets Writing thank-you letters Visiting seniors homes Saying thank-you more often to people who work in the community Going to garage sales

- Pass out the I Am a Community Member template on page 123. Invite students to choose one place in the community they visit often and feel that they benefit from. Invite them to think of one way they might be able to help in their own community.

Caring Community Inquiry: A Unit in Action

Parvina Panghali, exceptional primary teacher and Early Learning Team coach in SD 23 Central Okanagan, transformed this lesson on the community into a brilliant inquiry unit stemming from the students' question: "If we benefit so much from our community, why aren't we giving back?" The inquiry posed by her Grade 1 and 2 students centred around "connecting and contributing to our local community" and thinking of ways they might be able to help. Without an end goal in mind, she ventured out into the community with her students, exploring places and meeting people in person and online to see what they might discover. Their lived community experience included

- Local walks in the neighborhood
- Visits to local shops, the community garden, the local high school, and a local farm
- Talking to an agriculturalist, store owners, garbage collectors

During their explorations, they observed and looked for ways they might be able to contribute or work with the community to help in some way. On one of their walks, they noticed Bee Ambassador signs in some people's yards. Students asked what the signs meant, and after a Google search back in class, they discovered that their school was located on the Kelowna Nectar Trail, which supports the Bee Ambassador program. On further investigation, they discovered that their school had removed flowers from a section of the Nectar Trail that served the bees. This sparked an interest in learning about how bees use the nectar to make honey. Soon, the students began to realize that the decline of honeybees is a huge issue, both locally and globally, and felt responsible for the decline in the bee population due to the school's negligence. This ignited an idea to help the community by replanting the flowers on the Nectar Trail to help the bees.

Now that they had a goal, the students were completely committed and excited about their project. Parvina created a text set of bee books to share with the students. They learned about bees and the plants they needed, and visited a local bee farm to learn more about the honey-making process. They wrote letters to the community and were able to secure donations from Home Depot and support from family/friends to build garden boxes. They received donations of soil from a local farm, and donations of pollinator flowers to rebuild the Nectar Trail for the bees. On the day of planting, family and community members volunteered to help the students transform the garden space to support the bees. As part of their work to become champions of change in their community, the children also created 24 booklets to hand out to classes in the school, sharing their knowledge of honeybees and the importance of revitalizing the garden with all the students in the school. They went into each class, teaching them about the Nectar Trail, the bees, and their work. They also spent a great deal of time monitoring the the new garden to see if it has an impact on the bees.

Back in the day, students might have participated in a Social Studies unit on the community by coloring pictures of local community helpers and learning about and the jobs they do. Or maybe they would have worked on a fact-based Science unit on bees, in which they labeled the bee's body parts and learned the roles of the queen, workers, and drones in honey-making. Compare that to the depth this inspirational unit took, and to the knowledge-building and deep learning—not to mention exceptional pride—these students demonstrated. Well, there is no comparison. Those students were committed and engaged in their learning because an engaged teacher was committed to their learning.

My Community and Me

Name: _____

Draw a picture of yourself inside the small circle. In the outside circle, draw, label, and color places in your community.

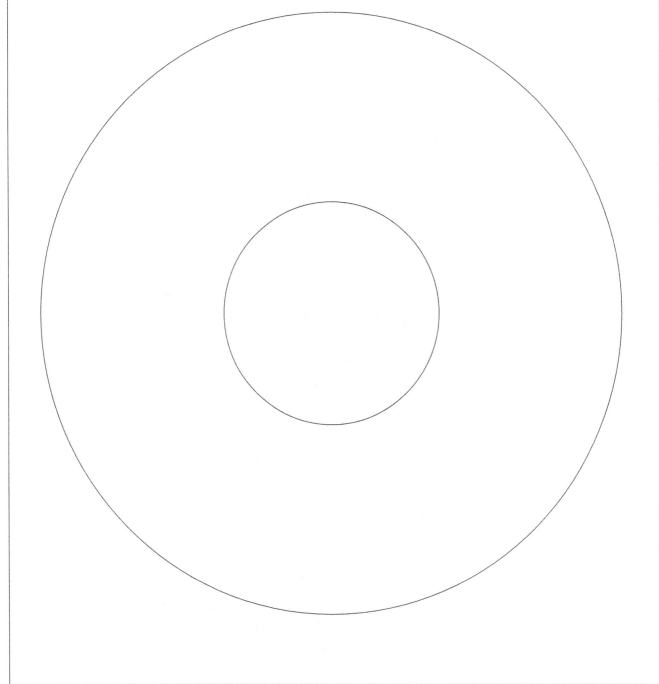

I Am a Community Member

Name: _____

My Community Helps Me Choose a place in your community you visit often. How does this place help you?	I Help My Community Choose one thing you can do to help your community. Draw and write how you will do this.
_____ _____ _____ _____ _____	_____ _____ _____ _____ _____

Pembroke Publishers ©2024 *Powerful Thinking* by Adrienne Gear ISBN 9781551383637

8 Thinking in Math

Kendra Jacobs, a numeracy specialist in the Central Okanagan school district, uses thinking and metacognition regularly in her math lessons. Many of the strategies she uses in her numeracy lessons share the metacognitive foundation that I use in Reading Power. She has generously shared these ideas with me and shown me how she has adapted some of the thinking into numeracy lessons. With her permission, this chapter is based on Kendra's expertise, ideas, and teaching practice.

Metacognition, the awareness and ability to think about our thinking, is extremely important in Math class. Metacognition helps children understand that math is about reasoning and thinking, not just memorizing facts or procedures to solve a problem. Kendra uses the same language of thinking we use in literacy lessons—connect, question, visualize, infer, and transform—in her math lessons to help children make sense of their thinking across all subjects. Using metacognitive strategies and language across subjects allows us to help children view them as holistic thinking opportunities instead of isolated silos of subject matter. It also helps make Math more meaningful and engaging.

Lesson: Connecting Thinking Powers to Math Talk

Kendra uses this short lesson early in the school year to help link thinking to Math as well as to build a caring Math community in her classroom.

Teaching the explicit reasons as to why we communicate helps to create a culture of thinking for all children, where every child's voice matters. Revisit this idea often at the start of your year, as you launch community math conversations. Students might not use all of the thinking powers just yet, but if we introduce them early, it will help build the language and connections across subjects, sending the message that we value thinking in our classroom. Once you have introduced this communication structure, you can use it for a variety of math routines throughout the year.

> When introducing the idea of number talks to her class, Kendra refers to them as "community math conversations."

- Begin the lesson:

  Mathematicians, today we are going to do a lot of important thinking. Let's get our thinking brains ready.

  (Hold your hand up to simulate a brain)

  Now, when we are thinking about Math, we are going to be making connections, asking questions, making inferences, visualizing, and transforming our thinking.

(As you say each thinking power, put down one finger at a time so that you end
with a closed fist)

- Continue the lesson:

> *Now, let's bring our hands to our hearts with our thumbs pointing up. Instead of
> raising your hand when you have an idea, I want you to show me with a silent
> thumbs-up against your heart.*

(Model the thumbs-up as you say this)

> *Why do you think we will use a thumbs-up to communicate, instead of a hand up?*

(Possible answers: tired arm, distracting for others to have
a hand waving in the air)

> *I wonder, does this ever happen to you? When you see someone else's hand up after
> the teacher asks a question, you think, "Oh they already have the answer so I'll just
> wait to see what they have to say." And you STOP thinking! We know that mathe-
> maticians do lots of thinking, so, together, let's make sure we don't stop anyone else's
> thinking. A thumbs-up on your heart shows you are thinking and being considerate
> of other thinkers in the class.*

Lesson: Change My Thinking

Math provides an excellent opportunity to bring thinking transformations to
life. One effective strategy to encourage this transformation is introducing the
concept of *Change My Thinking* (CMT). When you notice children erasing or
scribbling out their math mistakes, or when you explicitly teach the value of a
growth mindset and learning from errors, it's the perfect time to introduce this
lesson. When we publicly value changed thinking, through conversation and visible thinking, we send a powerful message to our students that thinking transformations are not only okay, but also encouraged and valued. This practice helps
children develop flexibility in their thinking, and you'll often notice it extending
beyond math—they may start using a simple line and *CT* throughout their writing and other subjects.

- Start the lesson by sharing with the class:

> *In this class, we value all kinds of thinking, including our mistakes! I've noticed that
> when some of you make math mistakes, you scribble them out. In our community,
> instead of erasing or scribbling your mistakes, I'd like you to draw a nice, neat line
> through them, and then put CT (for Changed Thinking) above them. Why do you
> think we would do that?*

Encourage responses and ideas from the children. You might even turn it into
a group discussion or turn and talk.

Common Student Responses and Teacher Comments

Child Response: *Because scribbles are messy, and we want our work to be neat.*

Teacher Comment: *Neat work is helpful, but what's more important than neatness
is your thinking. We know that thinking can be messy sometimes, right? That's why
mathematicians use one line.*

Child Response: *So we can keep our work organized.*

Teacher Comment: *Mathematicians are very organized, which is one reason they don't just scribble out their work.*

Child Response: *So we can see our mistakes.*

Teacher Comment: *Interesting, so are you saying if you put one neat line through your mistake, you can still see it? Why might that be helpful?*

(Encourage a turn-and-talk discussion)

- Continue the lesson:

  In our Math community, we know that learning from our mistakes is important. When we draw a neat line through our thinking, we can go back to it if we need to, because we can still see it. It also helps us remember that mistakes can help us learn. They don't need to slow us down by taking the time to scribble all over them. One quick line can help us keep thinking about the problem.

CHANGE MY THINKING EXTENSION

Consider reading *The Most Magnificent Thing* as a read-aloud. Ask students if they can make any connections to Math from the day before. Guide them toward the idea that there are connections between changed thinking and using past mistakes to create something magnificent.

TEACHER TIPS

- Model making your own mistakes (authentically and planned!) and drawing a neat line with the letters *CT* (Changed Thinking) above instead of erasing them. Do this repeatedly throughout the year, in Math and across other subjects.
- Observe which students are most comfortable with this strategy and are using it often, and which children are not. For those who are not using it, sit beside them and observe. Notice and praise when they change their thinking, making it a comfortable celebration for them.
- You can use changed thinking as an indicator of growth in thinking transformation and Math assessment.

Lesson: The Knew–New in Math

For more metacognitive Math strategies and lessons, visit Kendra Jacobs blog at Mathematizing 24.7: https://www.mathematizing247.com/blog

Kendra has adapted many lesson ideas from Reading Power to Math, demonstrating the value of thinking in all areas of the curriculum. In this lesson, she shares how she uses the Knew–New structure (see lesson on page 71) to help students make sense of using connections when working with problem strings. It can be used as part of a math talk, or for both formative and summative assessment. A *problem string* is a series of related problems, purposefully sequenced to help students construct mathematical relationships, that nudges them toward a major efficient mathematical strategy. Each problem is discussed and connections are made before a new one is added.

For more information on problem strings go to www.mathisfigureoutable.com/blog/problem-string

- Tell students that they will be practicing their mathematical thinking today using problem strings. Explain that a problem string is a string of math problems that are connected. Looking and talking about each question on the string one at a time can really help expand our thinking!

- Write the equation 10 × 4 on the board. Tell them that this is the first problem on the string. Ask students to raise their hands if they know what the answer is (depending on the grade, most will know).

- Tell students that knowing an answer is important, but thinking about how they got the answer is what you want to focus on (some will say "I just know it," but let that go!).

- Ask students to explain what the problem is asking. What are we trying to find out? (*If you have four groups of ten things, how many do you have?*) Illustrate this on the board using dots or sticks.

●●●●●●●●●●   ●●●●●●●●●●   ●●●●●●●●●●   ●●●●●●●●●●

Comment to students that multiplying is much easier than having to count all those dots!

- Explain you are now going to add another problem to the problem string. Write the equation 12 × 4 on the board. Tell students that you would like them to think about how the first problem at the top of the string, 10 × 4, might help them solve 12 × 4. Use some of these nudging questions to prompt the children:

  - *What do you already know that might help you solve this problem?*
  - *Can you break down the numbers to ones that you are familiar with?*
  - *What strategy can you use that might help you solve this problem?*
  - *Does this problem remind you of any other problems you have solved before?*

- When the children talk about facts and information they already know, it might sound something like this:

I already knew 10 × 4 equals 40.
I already knew that 12 is 2 more than 10.
I already knew that 4 × 2 is 8
Now I KNOW I can add 8 to 40 to solve the problem!

- Explicitly highlight this for them as a relevant and valued mathematical strategy.

So you are saying you already knew that 10 × 4 equals 40, and you used that to help you solve the new problem 12 × 4. Using what you know is a great way to help you solve math problems that you don't yet know!

This is an example of a problem string Kendra adapted from *Minilessons for Early Multiplication and Division* by Willem Uittenbogaard and Catherine Twomey Fosnot. Note that problems are written one at a time, horizontally; after each problem has been discussed, a new one is added on.

Problem string problem (write one at a time)	Prompting Thinking Questions You Might Ask	Notes to Notice
10×8	*Let's get out thinking brains ready. This is our first question. When you have an idea about this question, show me with a thumbs-up.*	• Prompt to thinking brain. • Starts with an entry point that all children are familiar with. • Record thinking visually with a number line.
11×8	*Here comes the next one. Show me with a thumbs-up. (Give thinking time) How did you solve this? So, you are saying you already knew 10×8 and you used that to help you solve 11×8? Using what you know is a great way to help you solve math problems that you don't yet know! Turn and talk: (Name), re-tell what strategy you just used. Can someone share (Name)'s strategy? I wonder if that strategy will be helpful for our next one?*	• Explicitly make the connection to the previous question if someone raises the idea that they used 10×8 and just added a group of 8. • If someone offers 88 as solved by "$11 \times$ anything is just two of the same digits," acknowledge that it is interesting, but don't linger or focus on that conversation.
9×8	*Here comes the next one. Show me with a thumbs up. (Give thinking time) How did you solve this? So you are saying you already knew 10×8 and you used that to help you solve 9×8? You just took away one group of 8? Interesting, so many connections to the problems we already know.*	• Again, focus on helping students connect to the 10×8 problem they already know. • Students might also offer up $9 \times 5 + 9 \times 3$ as a strategy to solve this. Here, we can still celebrate the connections to what they already know.
10×6 11×6 9×6	Repeat a similar sequence to above, highlight making connections to 10×6 and using what they know to help them solve new problems.	• Model this on a different number line, but leave the problem you used written on top so that, at the end, students can make connections between both number lines to clearly identify the strategy.

11×5	*Here is our last problem. This one is tricky! I wonder what you might use that you already know to help figure this one out.*	• Here, we are not providing the helper problem, but nudging students to make the connections on their own. This will be challenging for some, but some will very quickly use 10×5 to help them solve it.
	What an interesting string we solved today! We know that mathematicians are always thinking. What strategy connections are you making between the problems? What are you still wondering about?	• Prompt students to notice connections between the problems, as well as to wonder: *Will this strategy always work?* • If students are getting restless by the end, offer these final observation prompts as a stand-up-hand-up-pair-up variation of a turn and talk to get their bodies moving, but keep them on task.

This shows a portion of the number string used in this example. Note that the number string is accumulative, and new questions are added to the bottom of the sequence one at a time.

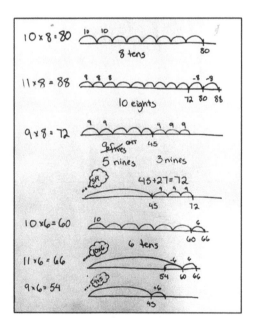

• At the end of the problem string, you might ask students to think about what new strategies they have discovered today:

Mathematicians, what new strategies did you learn today in our problem string? Turn and talk to your partner and share something that is new to you.

What strategies did we use today that you already knew and were familiar with? Turn and talk to your partner and share something we talked about today that you already knew a lot about.

Prompting this metacognition at the end of a problem string helps to create habits of thinking in children so that, when they are working independently, they have experience with these types of questions and reflections. This helps to build independent learners and thinkers in math and gives children access points for solving unfamiliar problems to them.

Sample of a student using the Knew–New structure as part of a formative assessment and reflections on a multiplication lesson. (See the Math Knew–New template on page 131.)

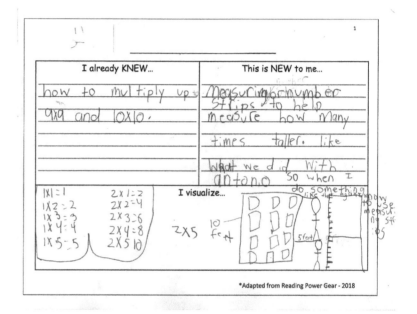

Math Knew–New

Name: _____

I already KNEW…

This is NEW to me…

I visualize…

9 Thinking in Art, Music, and Phys Ed

Thinking in Art

As I shared in the Introduction, watching an educator use Reading Power strategies in her Grade 5 Art class was a transformational moment for me.

Lesson: Thinking Deeply About Art

To help students begin to think more deeply about art, try weekly TDAA! (Think Deeply About Art!) lessons (see TDAA! template on page 134). Not only is this an excellent way to integrate thinking into a content lesson, but it is also a wonderful opportunity to introduce a variety of artistic styles, elements, principals, techniques, eras, and artists to your students. Even if you don't teach Art, these lessons are simple, with very little prep involved: just a quick search for an interesting art image to project and 10 to 15 minutes to look, think, and discuss.

- Post the image of a piece of art on the interactive whiteboard or screen. Some suggested art pieces for sharing:

  Classic Art
  Skedans by Emily Carr
  The Dance Class by Edward Degas
  Dawson City by Ted Harrison
  The Human Condition by Rene Magritte
  Composition with Yellow, Blue and Red by Piet Mondrian
  The Scream by Edvard Munch
  Red Poppy by Georgia O'Keefe
  Portrait of Dora Maar by Pablo Picasso
  The Raven and the First Men (sculpture) by Bill Reid
  Starry Night by Vincent Van Gogh
  Sunday on the Island of La Grande Jatte by George Seurat
  Mona Lisa by Leonardo da Vinci
  Campbell Soup Cans by Andy Warhol

  Contemporary Art
  Balloon Girl by Banksy
  Land of Dreams by Marcus Cadman
  Spirit by Tyree Guyton
  Pumpkin (or Mushroom) by Yayoi Kusama
  Sharing is Caring by Tyeb Mehta
  Man Changing into Thunderbird by Norval (Copper Thunderbird) Morrisseau
  Skulls and Flowers Blue by Takashi Murakami

Pow Wow Singers by Daphne Odjig
Lucky Mirror by Angel Otero
Something Vibrant by Jessi Raulet
Sparkling Dew on Spring Flowers by Alma Woodsey Thomas
Equestrian Portrait of Charles I by Kehinde Wiley
Syrian Migration (series) by Helen Zughaib

- Invite students to spend a few moments studying the art piece. While they look, ask them to pay attention to their thinking. Guide them through the painting with some open-ended questions:

  - *What did your eyes notice first in this painting? What were you first drawn to?*
  - *What are you wondering about this painting? About the painter who painted it?*
  - *What does this painting remind you of? What connections are you making?*
  - *What are you noticing that is interesting or surprising about the image?*
  - *Close your eyes for a moment and think about the painting. What stands out in your mind?*

- Use the Think for 1, Talk for 2, Share for 3 strategy (see page 24) to initiate a discussion about the painting. Invite students to share their thinking about the painting with partners and then with the class.
- The lesson can either end here or be used as a segue into an art activity.

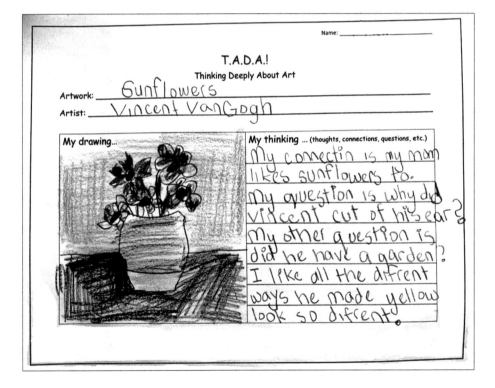

TDAA!
Thinking Deeply About Art

Name: _____

Artwork: _____

Artist: _____

My drawing

My thinking (thoughts, connections, questions, etc.)

Pembroke Publishers ©2024 *Powerful Thinking* by Adrienne Gear ISBN 9781551383637

Thinking in Music

Like Art, Music is a wonderful opportunity to engage students in thinking and talking about different pieces and styles. Again, even if you don't teach music or are not musically inclined, this is a effective way to introduce students to different types of music and to engage them in listening, thinking, and talking about what the music means to them.

Lesson: Thinking Deeply About Music

- Have students get comfortable, either at their desks or on the carpet, either sitting or lying down and closing their eyes. I recommend doing a few simple breathing exercises with them before playing the music, just to help them relax.
- Explain you are going to play a piece of music and that, while it is playing, you want them to listen and think about the music. When the music is over, they will have a chance to talk to a partner.
- While the music is playing, quietly pose these questions, giving time between each so the students can think:

  - *What does this music make you think about?*
  - *How does this music make you feel?*
  - *What pictures can you see in your mind while you are listening?*
  - *What are you wondering about this music?*
  - *What connections are you making?*
  - *What is something you notice or like about this piece of music?*

- After the music is finished playing, invite students to share their thinking with a partner. Alternatively, you can move directly into a whole-class discussion. Revisit the questions and invite students to share their thinking.
- Invite students to guess what they think the piece of music is called. Then tell students the name of the piece of music, the composer, and any background information you might wish to share; e.g., year, type of music, etc.
- Depending on the time you have, replay the music and invite students to draw a picture of what they see while they listen to the music, using the Musically Thinking template on page 138. If your students are familiar with Brain Pockets, explore the idea of drawing one picture from their Memory Pocket and another from their Imagination Pocket. You might use the Musical Brain Pockets template, page 139.

RECOMMENDED MUSIC

These pieces are recommended for listening/thinking lessons, starting with classical music and then moving into different types of music, some of which might stimulate a few dance moves! Most of the titles are easily available to stream. Some pieces are longer, so monitor your class and play only what you deem an appropriate length.

I have made every effort to ensure that the songs included are appropriate in both language and content, but please always listen first, as you know your students best.

Classical

"The Great Escape" theme by Elmer Bernstein (from the movie)
Water Music by Handel
Eine Kleine Nachtmusik by Mozart
"Canon in D Major" by Pachelbel

Peter and the Wolf by Prokofiev
"Flight of the Bumblebee" by Rimsky-Korsakov
Carnival of the Animals by Saint-Saëns
"The Beautiful Blue Danube" by Strauss
Swan Lake by Tchaikovsky
"Russian Dance" from *The Nutcracker* by Tchaikovsky
"Winter" from The Four Seasons by Vivaldi

Jazz

"What a Wonderful World" by Louis Armstrong
"Take Five" by the Dave Brubeck Quartet
"Blue Skies" by Ella Fitzgerald (or "A Tisket A Tasket")
"Linus and Lucy" (instrumental) by Vince Guaraldi Trio
"Fly Me to the Moon" by Frank Sinatra

Hip Hop

"Let The Bass Go" by Black Knight
"Motownphilly" by Boyz ll Men
"It's Just Begun" by Flying Funk
"Jump" by Kris Kross
"Old Town Road" by Lil Nas X featuring Billy Ray Cyrus
"How We Do" (from *Sponge Bob, the Movie*) by Snoop Dog, Monsta X

Folk

"Mr. Tambourine Man" by the Byrds
"Have You Ever Seen the Rain" by Creedance Clearwater Revival
"Blowin' in the Wind" by Bob Dylan
"This Land Is Your Land" by Woody Guthrie
"Big Yellow Taxi" by Joni Mitchell
"The Sound of Silence" by Simon and Garfunkel
"You've Got a Friend" by James Taylor

Country

"Ring of Fire" by Johnny Cash
"Crazy" by Patsy Cline
"Achy Breaky Heart" by Billy Ray Cyrus
"Take Me Home, Country Roads" by John Denver
"Where the Green Grass Grows" by Tim McGraw
"Jolene" by Dolly Parton
"Jambalaya" by Hank Williams

Early and Classic Rock and Roll

"Yellow Submarine" by the Beatles
"Johnny B. Goode" by Chuck Berry
"Splish Splash" by Bobby Darin
"I Love Rock and Roll" by Joan Jett
"Blue Suede Shoes" by Elvis Presley
"Born to Run" by Bruce Springsteen

I found a great list of music around the world on Spotify: Songs From Around the World (For All Children Across the World). I also found some great examples here: https://www.allaroundthisworld.com/listen/

Traditional Music from Around the World

Irish Jig (Ireland)

"Ulili E" (Hawaii)

First Nations drums (YouTube: Summer Solstice Festival Ottawa 2019, or Sound Healing Drum by Nazar Drums)

"Everyone Likes Calypso" (Caribbean)

"Troika" (Russia)

"Sur le Pont D'Avignon" (France)

"German Clapping Song" (Germany)

Schottische (Scotland)

Polka (Poland)

"Haru Ga Kita" (Japan)

"Pata Pata" (Africa)

"Take Me Out To The Ball Game" (U.S.A.)

"Planting Rice" (Philippines)

"Samba Parade" (Brazil)

"Chu Ech On" (Vietnam)

"Waltzing Matilda" (Australia)

"The Dreidel Song" (U.S.A., Israel)

"Lion Dance Song" (China)

"Cinco De Mayo" (Mexico)

"Diwali, Festival of Lights" (India)

Musically Thinking

Name: _____

When I listen to _____

it makes me think about _____

_____

_____

Musical Brain Pockets

Name: _____

Musical Piece: _____

Composer: _____

Memory Pocket	Imagination Pocket
_____	_____
_____	_____
_____	_____
_____	_____
_____	_____
_____	_____

Thinking in Phys Ed

Thinking in gym class? Don't panic! I'm not suggesting that students pause in the middle of their dodgeball game to share a connection! But I am sharing an idea to have your students practice visualizing before launching into an activity. In sports, visualization, or mental imagery, is a known practice of conditioning your brain for successful outcomes. The more you mentally rehearse your performance, the more it becomes habituated in your mind.

My son still talks about a hockey coach he had years ago who, before a game, took the players through a pre-game visualizing exercise. While "Thunderstruck" could be heard blasting from the walls of the opposing team's dressing room next door, my son's team, dressed and game ready, sat silently, visualizing, while the coach quietly talked them thorough opening puck drop—where they would stand, where they would be looking, their stick position, who they would be passing to, and their focus on the puck. My son was far more focused and far less anxious when he skated onto the ice that year than any year afterwards.

We have all experienced the "Thunderstruck" of gym time, the frenzy of noise and excitement when your class enters the gymnasium. Spending five minutes at the beginning of your gym activity engaging your students in a quiet visualizing exercise not only stimulates their thinking, but also helps them settle and focus more effectively than blowing a whistle would.

Lesson: Visualizing

Note: this exercise is intended to be used with a game or activity the students are already familiar with.

- Invite students to find a spot on the gym floor. Give them the option of sitting or lying down if you have mats.
- Invite them to close their eyes and talk them through a few deep breaths.

> *Today in gym, we are going to be playing _____. Before we get going, I would like you to spend a few minutes practicing visualizing. Remember, visualizing is something that can help us understand what we are thinking more clearly. If we can see it in our minds, it becomes clearer."*

Remind them that, when they visualize, the only part of their body that should be moving is their brain!

You may need to adjust the language of these prompts slightly, depending on the activity you are doing.

- Begin talking them through a short visualizing exercise, no more than three to five minutes. Pause between each comment to allow time for thinking. Speak in a quiet voice.

> *First, I would like you to think about the objective of the actual game. What is your goal or what are you trying to do? What do you need to do to achieve that goal? What might prevent you from achieving the goal? Who will you need to help you achieve the goal? Will you be working alone or with another person or group?*

> *Next, I would like you to think about where you will be standing in the gym. Visualize yourself there. Now, I'd like you to focus on your body and the physical actions you will need to use to play this game. What will your body be doing? Start with your feet. Visualize your feet in action. Now visualize your hands. What will your hands be doing? Visualize your hands in action. Now visualize your eyes. What will your eyes be focused on?*

Now visualize yourself in action in the middle of the game. What are you doing?
Now think about the end of the game. Did you reach your goal?

- Depending on your time, you might invite a few students to share their ideas about the goal of the game, what might prevent them from reaching the goal, and what their hands, feet, and eyes might be doing.
- Tell students to stand and quietly move to find their starting spot. Remind them to keep thinking about what they visualized as they begin to play.

10   Building Indigenous Knowledge in an Early Primary Classroom: A Unit in Action

> One of the most rewarding parts of my job is having the opportunity to visit a variety of schools and classrooms across the province of British Columbia. This past fall, I had the pleasure of sitting down with Staci Palahniuk and Carolyn Bassett-Smith, two exceptional early primary teachers from North Glenmore Elementary school in the Central Okanagan school district. With their permission, I am sharing their year-long plan to help their students build knowledge and deepen their understanding about Indigenous peoples of Canada. To me, it is an outstanding example of how to embed knowledge-building through interactive content-rich read-alouds and connected conversations in a primary classroom.

In 2016, the provincial curriculum in British Columbia went through a significant redesign. Among the many changes, the integration of Indigenous culture and perspectives throughout all areas of learning, at every grade level, and in every subject, was among the most significant. Up until that time, content about Indigenous peoples of Canada was regarded as a subject taught in Grade 4 or 5 Social Studies and, unless you taught that grade level, the likelihood of weaving Indigenous content into your teaching was minimal.

Many teachers, including myself, faced a huge learning curve. Few of us were Indigenous, so that, in and of itself, became a challenge. Many didn't necessarily feel qualified to be deliverers of this information, so we sought ways to be authentic and respectful about the material and content we were bringing into our classrooms. In terms of resources, there weren't many children's books in 2016 that would be classed today as authentically Indigenous; i.e., written by Indigenous authors. In terms of knowledge, many of us were in a beginning place in terms of our own understanding and knowledge of Indigenous beliefs and perspectives. Orange Shirt Day, for example, had not yet been established. Since 2016, a lot of work has been done in schools to respectfully build Indigenous knowledge and to decolonize our practice. Indigenous Advocates have been working in schools, supporting teachers and students in their learning. There are more and more Indigenous educational resources being developed to support the learning, and a huge surge of authentic Indigenous children's literature is being published and is becoming available to use in our classrooms.

A few years ago, Carolyn Bassett-Smith and Staci Palahniuk had set a goal for themselves, through their school growth plan, to look for ways to authentically and respectfully Indigenize their practice in the Grade 1 curriculum. An important consideration during their early discussions was not restricting their

Indigenous learning to a one-and-done lesson—on Orange Shirt Day, for example. Instead, they were looking for more of a "sprinkle" approach, seeking out ways to integrate an Indigenous learning journey for their students, hoping to build understanding across all subjects throughout their year. Not being Indigenous themselves, they knew and respected the importance of authenticity. And so, they turned to books. They spent long hours gathering a rich text set of authentic Indigenous picture books and information books, written by Indigenous Canadian authors. They looked for ways the books could be woven into their units of study: self, family, friendship, and cultural traditions, as well as Math, Art, and Music. They used these books, along with other non-Indigenous books, to provide an access point for the knowledge-building, and allowed time for students to share their thinking about the stories after each read-aloud. Conversations were rich and thoughtful, and took precedence over written responses.

Both Staci and Carolyn admitted they were nervous at the beginning; not being Indigenous themselves, they didn't want to get it wrong or "say it wrong." But being learners alongside their students, some of whom were Indigenous, being open and vulnerable about not knowing all the information, turned out to be one of the most effective and rewarding parts of their journey. They commented on how often they read and shared the author backnotes in the books they read, modeling to the students how they were building knowledge together. When reading books with Cree or Métis words included, for example, they sourced online sites that offered First-voice pronunciation of Indigenous words in the different dialects and played them for students to hear. They invited their school Indigenous Advocate, who was Métis, into their classrooms to share her culture with students through stories and activities, including sharing some of her beading work during their math patterning unit.

In reflecting on the year, they both agreed that it had been a huge learning curve for both them and for their students, but that the experience had been very rewarding. Both agreed that the authentic Indigenous books they used had been instrumental in helping them navigate their way into important topics with their Grade 1 students and provide an access point into the learning. As well as integrating Indigenous content into curriculum topics, the books were also excellent starting places for students to think and talk about such issues as Residential Schools, Orange Shirt Day, Truth and Reconciliation, and Earth Day. Both teachers were surprised, in fact, how simple and natural it was to weave Indigenous books into their units of study, rather than try to design a new Indigenous unit around a book. Finally, both said how valued their work had been and how much depth, knowledge, and understanding their students came away with.

> It is our job as teachers to set kids on a path of knowing, wondering, and caring deeply about others. It is our job to commit to reconciliation and to teach our students what that means. Even [Grade 1 students] need to understand that terrible things have happened to Indigenous people in our country. Even [Grade 1 students] can understand it was a not a good idea to send family members away to bad schools. Unless we do the hard work and introspection ourselves, unless we try to do better to decolonize and Indigenize our curriculum, nothing will change. We were committed to doing this work, we collaborated, we planned together, we learned together, we made lots of mistakes along the way—but we DID see and feel a change happening in our students. We feel very proud of that. (Carolyn Bassett-Smith and Staci Palahniuk, 2023)

"The Power of sharing words is not only in what is written or spoken. There is also power in how words are received: in how a person takes them in, turns them over, assesses them for authenticity, and transforms then into their lived experience." – Jo Chrona, *Wayi Wah!* (page 6)

"In talking with a number of Indigenous Advocates over the years, I have learned that they often feel pressured to be experts on Indigenous culture, when many of them are just starting to learn more about their own cultures, due to the intergenerational effects of residential schools. Often, they are busy with student needs and don't have time to create or present cultural lessons for classrooms. I think it's important that non-Indigenous classroom teachers not place an unfair burden of responsibility on their school's Indigenous Advocate, but rather do their own background work and planning, and then ask if the Advocate is available/interested in co-teaching or sharing anything to enhance what the teacher is already doing." — Carolyn Bassett-Smith

One important note Carolyn gave me was that, before each read-aloud, they would always try to make special reference to the Indigenous author and illustrator of the book they were sharing, often reading aloud the about-the-author and about-the-illustrator bios from the back cover, as well as any backnotes the author provided. Before beginning the story, they would also provide a short Book Bite (see lesson on page 67) to provide context, vocabulary, and connections for the students. After the read-aloud, they would include a short reflection time, when students would think, talk to a partner, then share their thoughts, feelings, questions, connections, etc. about the book with the class. Both she and Staci agreed that this was often when they noticed rich learning and discussions unfolding. After reading *Phyllis's Orange Shirt* by Phyllis Webstad, one student commented, "But it's not really fair that the kids had to go to a school they didn't want to go to. Why did they have to go?"

Staci and Carolyn's year-long growth plan to build knowledge and understanding of Indigenous beliefs and perspectives into their Grade 1 curriculum using authentic Indigenous picture books is summarized in this outline (used and adapted with permission). It's important to note that non-Indigenous anchor books were included in these units of studies, alongside the Indigenous titles listed in the plan, but are not listed on this plan.

SEPTEMBER

Introduce *Indigenous*

- Video: "What is Indigenous?" CBC Kids
  - Excellent explanation of First Peoples (living in a place) and introduction to the four Canadian Indigenous Groups: First Nations, Cree, Metis, Inuit

Class Community Building

- Share a variety of picture books to support positive class community
- Anchor Books: *Our Class Is a Family* by Shannon Olsen
  The Sharing Circle by Theresa Larsen-Jonasson
  The Sharing Circle by Theresa Meuse-Dallien (chapter 1)
- Invite Indigenous Advocate to facilitate class sharing circle

Who Am I?

- Building positive self-identity, appreciation for unique characteristics (outside, inside, talents, name, family, culture)
- Teacher Resource: *Powerful Understanding* (SELF) by Adrienne Gear
- Anchor Book: *Thunder Boy Jr.* by Sherman Alexie

Math: Patterning

- Link to patterns in beading
- Anchor Book: *We Can Bead* by Nadine McSpadden
  Link: https://schmedia.pearsoncanada.ca/mlb/book.html?code=KP2&batch=B3
  - Activity: We Can Bead
- Article: CBC Kids info about Indigenous beading
  Link: https://www.cbc.ca/kids/articles/do-you-know-what-beading-is
  Art: use wooden beads and elastic to make a patterned bracelet

Truth and Reconciliation Week

- Anchor Book: *Phyllis's Orange Shirt* by Phyllis Webstad (Primary version)
  - Video: CBC Video *"What is Orange Shirt Day?"* featuring Phyllis Webstad
- Anchor Book: *Our Orange Hearts* by Phyllis Webstad (also available on YouTube)
  - **Art:** Design a paper orange shirt (provide orange heart shaped punch-outs and template)
- Anchor Book: *When We Were Alone* by David A. Robertson (Cree Characters)
  - Read and discuss book. Then prompt "At school, children should feel…" Record responses on chart paper or on feathers template and display.
- Anchor Book: *When We Are Kind* by Monique Gray Smith

OCTOBER

Thanksgiving

- Share anchor books focusing on what we feel grateful and thankful for.
- Anchor Book: *Giving Thanks: A Native American Good Morning Message* by Chief Jake Swamp
  - Discuss Indigenous acknowledgment and appreciation of the land
  - Go on a Gratitude Walk outside around the school and give thanks to nature and the land. Back inside, draw and write about what they gave thanks for.

Math: Numbers to 10

- Anchor Books: *Acorns for Wilaya* by Nadine McSpadden
  We All Count: A Book of Ojibway Art by Jason Adair
  We All Count: A Book of Cree Numbers by Julie Flett
  Powwow Counting in Cree by Penny M. Thomas
- Website: First Voices website to teach counting from one to five in local Indigenous language (Syilx)

NOVEMBER

Social Emotional Learning: Friendship

- Teacher Resource: *Powerful Understanding* by Adrienne Gear (pages 95–104)
- Anchor Book: *You Hold Me Up* by Monique Gray Smith
  - Discuss ways you can support a friend or family member

How-To Writing

- Teacher Resource: *Powerful Writing Structures* by Adrienne Gear
- Anchor Books: *Mom, How Do You Make Smoked Fish?* by Celestine Aleck
  I Build an Igloo by Michael Kusugak
  Grandpa, How Do I Build an Iglu? Nunavummi Reading Series
  - Students choose a how-to topic to draw and write

DECEMBER

Art: Metis Mittens

- Anchor Book: *Metis Christmas Mittens* by Leah Marie Dorian

JANUARY

New Years

Social Studies: Family and Family Celebrations
- Anchor Book: *Métis New Year* by Leah Marie Dorian
- Anchor Books: *Trapline* by David A. Robertson
  Just Like Grandma by Kim Rogers
  - Discuss importance of grandparents and their role in our lives, what we can learn from them

Powwows

- Book link: *Sharing our Stories* – highlights the powwow as a celebration
  https://schmedia.pearsoncanada.ca/mlb/index.html?code=2G3
- Anchor Books: *Powwow Day* by Traci Sorell
  Jingle Dancer by Cynthia L. Smith
  Celebrating the Powwow by Bobbie Kalman
- Links: CBC Kids info about powwows
  https://www.cbc.ca/kidscbc2/the-feed/do-you-know-what-a-powwow-is
  and regalia
  https://www.cbc.ca/kidscbc2/the-feed/do-you-know-what-regalia-is

FEBRUARY/MARCH

- Kamik Series Read-Alouds
  Kamik: An Inuit Puppy Story
  Kamik's First Sled
  Kamik Joins the Pack
  Kamik takes the Lead

Social Studies: Family and Family/Cultural Celebrations
- Anchor Books: *P'esk'a and the First Salmon Ceremony* by Scot Ritchie
  Dipnetting with Dad by Willie Sellars
  Link: Video of author Willie Sellars and Illustrator talking about the book
  https://www.youtube.com/watch?v=IUoDcWOJ9ww

APRIL

Earth Day (Month)

- Anchor Books: *We are Water Protectors* by Carole Lindstrom
  The Water Walker by Joanne Robertson
  Autumn Peltier: Water Warrior by Carole Lindstrom

Science: Seasonal Changes (Spring)

  Anchor Books: *Forever Our Home* by Tonya Simpson
  It's Time for Berries! by Jeremy Debikki

Math

- *Let's Play Waltes* (Mathology): A counting game
  Book Link: https://schmedia.pearsoncanada.ca/mlb/book.
  html?code=K6SE&batch=B1
  - Use set of wood bowls, buttons, and sticks for students to play the game

MAY

Science: Plants

- Anchor Books: *A Day With Yayah* by Nicola Campbell
  Berry Song by Micheala Goulde
  A Walk on the Tundra by Rebecca Hainnu
  A Walk on the Shoreline by Rebecca Hainnu

Nature Walk

- Anchor Book: *Walking Together* by Elder Albert D. Marshall
  - Plant Cards for Nature Walk (from *A Day With Yayah* by Nicola Campbell)
    https://bcaitc.ca/sites/default/files/resources/Wild%20Plant%20Cards.pdf

Art: Métis Dandelion Art

- Anchor Book: *Âmî Osâwâpikones /Dear Dandelion* by SJ Okemow
- Art Link: Dandelion Puffs https://artroombritt.blogspot.com/2018/06/
  dandelion-puffs.html?m=0

JUNE

- ### Science: Objects in the Sky

Anchor Books: *We Learn from the Sun* by David Bouchard
Tann's Moons by Alison Gear (yes, that's my sister!)
Thirteen Moons on Turtle's Back by Joseph Bruchac
Raven: A Trickster Tale from the Pacific Northwest by Gerald McDermott: Compare
  story to *Grandfather Twilight* by Barbara Berger:
  - Raven putting the sun in the sky and Grandfather Twilight putting the
    moon in the sky. Discuss beliefs and appreciating that various cultures have
    different stories.
- Art Link: Raven Collages https://myadventuresinpositivespace.blogspot.
  com/2011/12/raven-collages.html

Final Thoughts

During a recent walk with my good friend Lisa, she replayed a conversation she had had with her son Simon a few weeks after he began his first year at university. He is passionate about health and fitness and had started his degree in a Kinesiology program.

> Lisa: *So how have the first few weeks been for you? How does it compare to high school, do you think?*
>
> Simon: *You know in high school, Mom, most of the classes are boring and you are just doing the work but don't really care about it much. And then you get a teacher who gives you a project you are really interested in and, all of a sudden, you get excited and can't wait to work on it at home and maybe you and your buddy are doing it together and it's all you talk about? Well, university is like that—all the time!*

Granted, Simon had the benefit of finding his passion early in life and starting a program completely aligned with that passion. Such is not the case for every first-year university student. But my point is this: when students are excited about learning, when they feel a little fire flickering inside their head and their heart, they are far more likely to be engaged and pursue the journey—to keep learning, keep thinking, keep wondering, keep connecting, keep talking. It is as simple and complex as that. Yes, the content needs to be taught and not every child is going to be excited about every topic. But let's step up to the challenge and do our best to make content learning interesting, exciting, and engaging for our students. Our students don't need us for facts; one quick swipe and they have more than enough facts to fill their heads. What they do need from us is an access point into their thinking. Think of it in terms of a thinking ticket—a ticket we provide every student, a ticket that comes complete with engagement, motivation, inspiration, and a good nudge to help them get past the literal facts and build the knowledge they need to understand the world a little better. You are their ticket into thinking.

In summary, I leave you with a list (I love lists!) to help you get started passing out those tickets!

- Create a culture of thinking in your class—make thinking visible!
- Model your thinking as often as you can.
- Be excited about the subjects you are teaching. Excitement breeds excitement.
- Be a learner alongside your students.
- Gather and share a wide range of content-rich nonfiction texts in your class.
- Engage in regular interactive read-alouds using content-rich texts.

- Engage learners in regular interactive conversations, both with partners and with the class.
- Help students build knowledge and vocabulary by reading collections of books on the same topic.
- Nudge your learners from re-telling toward re-thinking.
- Ask prompting questions to help stretch and extend students' thinking.
- Lean in and listen to your students talking. They might surprise you!

And if the list seems a little overwhelming, here is a simple step-by-step plan:

1. Find an interesting book connected to a subject you are teaching. (See booklists on pages 50–54, 76, 84, 95, 97, 99–100, 107–108, 111–112, 118, and 119.)
2. Prepare and share a Book Bite of key vocabulary and context (see page 67).
3. Read the book aloud to your class. Be excited about it! (See *interactive reading* on page 54.)
4. Share your brain reading while you book read (see page 22 for *brain reading* and *book reading*).
5. Invite students to share their thinking: Think for 1, Talk for 2, Share for 3 (see page 24).
6. Reflect on the story, the knowledge building, the thinking with a lesson (see pages 58–84).
7. Repeat.

You might have wished I started the book out with this list, it would have saved you a lot of time!

As a writer, my goal is to "gift" you, my readers, with something interesting, grounded in research, simple, and applicable to your teaching practice. I hope that this book has been that gift—a Knew–New of sorts—reinforcing things you already *knew* but also stretching your thinking about *new* ways to support every student in your class to develop into powerful thinkers.

A few weeks ago, I was commiserating with a good teacher friend (one of my literacy soul sisters). She was expressing her frustration at how toxic and exhausting the literacy world has become of late and how, some days, it makes her just want to throw in the towel. I connected, understanding first-hand her concerns, having been on the receiving end, on more than one occasion over the past few years, of the shaming and blaming that is happening daily in the elementary reading world. But my feeling is this—you can't please everyone. I know not everyone will be excitedly reading through to the end of this book, with sticky notes and highlighter pens in hand. In fact, some will see my name, roll their eyes, and not even open the cover! But after almost 30 years in this field, I will continue to fight for what I believe in.

So, my reader, remember this. What we do matters. And while there will always be nay-sayers questioning our practice, let us stand firm in our belief: rigid, scripted programs and worksheets do not promote knowledge building, powerful thinking, or joyful learning. Every learner deserves to have foundational instruction in both book reading and brain reading. Every learner deserves to be in a classroom where knowledge building, vocabulary, and comprehension are at the forefront of their learning. Every learner deserves the chance to engage in content-rich texts and interactive read-alouds. Every learner deserves real books, in their hands and in their hearts. Above all else, all learners deserve to see themselves as powerful readers and thinkers.

Dear teachers, thank you for reading this book. Thank you for embracing this profession with an open heart and an open mind. Thank you for gifting your students with a rich literacy life they will carry with them into the world. My gratitude for your dedication is immeasurable.

Acknowledgments

My book acknowledgments, over the course of many books, have been the source of amusement for some, as they often take up more pages than my Preface. But writing a book is not a solo enterprise and this is my opportunity to acknowledge those who have supported me through these pages.

Writing a book is not easy. (I equate it to giving birth. Had I remembered the labor, I might only have had one! This is my ninth book, so my memory must be terrible!) Writing a book on the side of a busy schedule of workshops, webinars, travel, blog posts, book reading and reviewing, not to mention wifing, mothering, sistering, and friending, is even more challenging. Throw in an end-of-summer deadline during a summer of visitors, unexpected losses, fires, and evacuations, and you know why this one took a little longer to complete! I could not have written this without the help of my family, friends, and colleagues, who encouraged me, supported me, and cheered me on to the finish line.

First, to my dear friends Cheryl Burian, Heather Barry, Donna Boardman, Jennifer Gordon, Kathleeen Keeler, Donna Kozak, Kimberly Matterson, Katie McCormack, Kimberly Stacey, Sue Stevenson, Lisa Wilson, and Amy Wou: my deepest gratitude. Having you in my life just makes my life better. I am eternally grateful for the hikes, dog walks, talks, texts, phone calls, cups of tea, glasses of wine, heart-to-hearts, book discussions, "teacher talks," card games, pie-making, apartment hunting, trip planning, lake swimming, movie nights, pedicure dates, dinner parties, princess-and-the-pea sleepovers, and many laughs and tears we have shared along the way.

Always, an extra-special thank-you to my dearest, longest-held friend and biggest supporter, Cheryl, who proudly pitched this book idea to my publisher (and me!) over dinner last year at the *Reading For The Love Of It* conference in Toronto. Despite a most challenging and heart-breaking year, she continued to support me, and cheer me on, and never doubted my ability to complete this book. The *Shouldn't you be writing???!* texts did not go unnoticed. Love you with all my heart, dearest friend.

To my late parents, Irv and Sheila Gear: the extraordinary gifts you gave me are woven into every fabric of my life. I am a better teacher, mother, wife, friend, reader, writer, hiker, baker, dog-lover, and "gifter" because of you. To my dearest sisters, Alison and Janet—both writers and teachers themselves—for your loving kindness every day. While we don't see each as often as I would like (like every day!), our bond is unbreakable and you are my family to the end.

To my dear friends and colleagues at J.W. Sexsmith Elementary in Vancouver: while I may not be there in person anymore, a piece of my heart always will be. I miss you, the students, and that school every day. To my current colleagues, Colleen Keeler and Hayley Legassie, you have helped tremendously with the "back end" of my business and helped me streamline my work so that I could focus on my writing. I am so grateful to you both and could not have managed without you.

To the exceptional educators of SD 23, who have opened up their schools, classrooms, and kitchens, generously supported my efforts, and provided me not only with extraordinary insight and guidance, but also with inspirational lessons and research to include in this book—Parvina Panghali, Donna Kozak, Lisa Wilson, Sue Stevenson, Kendra Jacobs, Staci Palahniuk, and Carolyn Bassett-Smith: my enormous gratitude for your generosity of spirit and exceptional practice. My thinking stretches every time I'm in your company.

To my steadfast editor Kat: it has been a great privilege to have worked with you through each of my books. You have an amazing gift of helping me find the thread: I could not have written this book, or any of my books for that matter, without you. To Mary Macchiusi, my publisher and friend, and the entire Pembroke team: thank you for continuing to support my work and for your patience through my many unexpected delays and summer roadblocks. When my deadline came and went, you offered only kindness and encouragement. A huge thank-you to all.

To my husband, Richard, for his quiet concessions and endless cups of coffee, for picking up the pieces that my book-writing self leaves behind, and for giving me the space and place to finish this one: I could not have managed without you. My deepest appreciation and love. And finally, to my dearest boys Spencer and Oliver: your unwavering love, belief, and encouragement made the hard parts easier. There are no triple-scoop words big enough to hold my love.

Professional Resources

Anderson, R.C., and Pearson, P.D. (1984). "A schema-theoretic view of basic processes in reading comprehension" In P. D. Pearson (ed.), *Handbook of Reading Research* (255–291). New York, NY: Longman.

Bailey, D.H., Duncan, G.J., Cunha, F., Foorman B.R., and Yeager, D.S. (2020). "Persistence and fade-out of educational-intervention effects: Mechanisms and potential solutions" *Psychological Science in the Public Interest,* 21 (2), 55–97. https://doi.org/10.1177/1529100620915848

Baker, L., and Brown, A.L. (1984). "Metacognitive skills and reading" In P. D. Pearson, R. Barr, M.L. Kamil and P. Mosenthal (eds.), *Handbook of Reading Research* (353–394). New York, NY: Longman.

Bogaerds-Hazenberg, Suzanne, Evers-Vermeul, Jacqueline, and van den Bergh, Huub (2021). "A meta-analysis on the effects of text structure instruction on reading comprehension in the upper elementary grades" *Reading Research Quarterly* 56 (3), July/August/September, 435–462.

Cabell, Sonia Q, and Hwang, HyeJin (2020) "Building content knowledge to boost comprehension in the primary grades" Reading Research Quarterly 55 (S1), S99–S107.

Cervetti, G.N., and Hiebert, E.H. (2018). "Knowledge at the center of English/Language Arts instruction. *The Reading Teacher* 72(4).

Chrona, Jo (2022). *Wayi Wah!: Indigenous Pedagogies: An Act for Reconciliation and Anti-Racist Education.* Winnipeg, MN. Portage and Main.

Clark, Christina, and Teravainen-Goff, Anne (2020). *Children and Young People's Reading in 2019: Findings from Our Annual Literacy Survey.* National Literacy Trust Research Report.

Correia, M.P. (2011). "Fiction vs. Informational Texts: Which will kindergartners choose?" *Young Children,* 66, 100–104.

Davis, M. (2006). *Reading Instruction: The Two Keys.* Charlottesville, VA: Core Knowledge Foundation.

Dole, J., Duffy, G., Roehler, L., and Pearson, P.D. (1991). "Moving From the Old to the New: Research on reading comprehension instruction" *Review of Educational Research,* 61 (2), 239–264.

Dougherty Stahl, K.A. (2011). "Applying new visions of reading development in today's classrooms" *The Reading Teacher: A Journal of Research-Based Classroom Practice,* 65 (1), 52–56.

Duke, Nell K. and Pearson, P. David (2002). "Effective practices for developing reading comprehension." In *What Research has to Say About Reading Instruction,* 3rd ed., edited by A.E. Farstrup and S.J. Samuels. Newark, DE: International Reading Association.

Duke, Nell K., Pearson, P. David, Strachan, Stephanie L., and Billman, Allison K. (2011). "Essential elements of fostering teaching reading comprehension" in S.J. Samuels and A.E. Farstrup (eds.) *What Research Has to Say About Reading Instruction*, 4th ed. Newark, DE: International Reading Association.

Duke, Nell K., and Cartwright, Kelly B. (2021). "The science of reading progresses: Communicating advances beyond the simple view of reading" *Research Quarterly,* 56 (S1).

Duke, N.K., Ward, A.E., & Pearson, P.D. (2021). "The science of reading comprehension instruction" *The Reading Teacher*, 74 (6), 663– 672.

Fisher, Douglas, Frey, Nancy, and Akhavan, Nancy (2019). *This is Balanced Literacy, Grades K–6*. Thousand Oaks, CA: Corwin Press.

Goldenberg, C. (1991). "Instructional conversations and their classroom applications" NCRCDSLL Educational Practice Reports. UC Berkeley: Center for Research on Education, Diversity and Excellence. https://escholarship. org/uc/item/6q72k3k9

Gonzalez, N., Moll, L.C., & Amanti, C. (2005) *Funds of Knowledge Theorizing Practices in Households, Communities, and Classrooms*. New York, NY: Routledge.

Goudvis, Anne, and Harvey, Stephanie (1998). *Nonfiction Matters: Reading, Writing, and Reseasrch in Grades 3–8.* Portland, ME: Stenhouse Publishers.

Goudvis, Anne, Harvey, Stephanie, and Buhrow, Brad (2019). *Inquiry Illuminated: Researchers Workshop Across the Curriculum.* Portsmouth, NH: Heinmann.

Gough, P.B., and Tunmer, W.E. (1986). "Decoding, reading, and reading disability *Remedial and Special Education*, 7, 6–10.

Heilman, A.W., Blair, T.R., and Rupley, W.R. (1998). *Principles and Practices of Teaching Reading*. Upper Saddle River, NJ: Merrill/Prentice-Hall.

Hwang, H., Lupo, S.M., Cabell, S.Q., and Wang, S. (2021). "What research says about leveraging the literacy block for learning. *Reading In Virginia*, XLII (2020–2021), 35-48. https://heyzine.com/flip-book/cf84416713.html

Ives, C.D., Freeth, R., and Fischer, J. (2020). "Inside-out Sustainability: The neglect of inner worlds" *Ambio* 49, 208–217.

Keene, Ellin Oliver (2018). *Engaging Children: Igniting a Drive for Deeper Learning K–9.* Portsmouth, NH: Heinmann

Keene, Ellin Oliver (2007). *Mosaic of Thought: The Power of Comprehension Strategy Instruction*, 2nd ed. Portsmouth, NH: Heinemann.

Kelly, Jennifer (2023). *Active Reading Classrooms.* Markham, ON: Pembroke Publishers

Kendeou, P., & van den Broek, P. (2007). "The effects of prior knowledge and text structure on comprehension processes during reading of scientific texts" *Memory & Cognition, 35* (7), 1567–1577.

Meyer, B.J.F., & Rice, G.E. (1984). "The structure of text" In P. D. Pearson, R. Barr, M. L. Kamil, & P. Mosenthal (eds.), *Handbook of Reading Research* (319–351). New York, NY: Longman.

Munger, Kristen A. (2016). *Steps to Success: Crossing the Bridge Between Literacy Research and Practice.* SUNY Online.

Nichols, Maria. *Building Bigger Ideas: A Process for Teaching Purposeful Talk.* Portsmouth, NH: Heinemann.

Paris, S.G., Wasik, B.A., and Turner, J.C. (1991). "The Development of Strategies of Readers" in R. Barr, M. Kamil, P. Mosenthal, & P. D. Pearson (eds.), *Handbook of Reading Research* Vol. 2 (609–640). Mahwah, NJ: Lawrence Erlbaum Associates.

Pearson, P. David (ed.) (2016). *Handbook of Reading Research*. New York, NY: Longman.

Piasta, S.B., Justice, L.M., McGinty, A.S., & Kaderavek, J.N. (2012). "Increasing young children's contact with print during shared reading: Longitudinal effects on literacy achievement" *Child Development*, 83 (3), 810–820.

Routman, Regie (2024). *The Heart-Centered Teacher: Restoring Hope, Joy, and Possibility in Uncertain Times*. New York, NY: Routledge.

Scarborough, H. S. (2002). "Connecting early language and literacy to later reading (dis)abilities: Evidence, theory, and practice" in S. B. Neuman & D. K. Dickinson (eds.), *Handbook of Early Literacy Research* (97–110). New York, NY: Guilford Press.

Smith, R., Snow, P., Serry, T., and Hammond, L. (2021). "The role of background knowledge in reading comprehension: A critical review" *Reading Psychology*, 42(3), 214–240.

Smolkin, L.B., & Donovan, C.A. (2001). "The contexts of comprehension: The information book read aloud, comprehension acquisition, and comprehension instruction in a first-grade classroom" *The Elementary School Journal*, 102 (2), 97–122.

Stewart, M. (ed.) (2020). *Nonfiction Writers Dig Deep: 50 award-winning authors share the secret of engaging writing*. NCTE.

Stewart, M., and Correia, M. (2021). *5 Kinds of Nonfiction: Enriching Reading and Writing Instruction with Children's Books*. Portland, ME: Stenhouse Publishers.

Strachan, Stephanie L. (2015). "Kindergarten students' social studies and content literacy learning from interactive read-alouds" *The Journal of Social Studies Research*, 39 (4), October, 207–223.

Willingham, D.T. (2017). "How to get your mind to read" *New York Times*, November 25. https://www.nytimes.com/2017/11/25/opinion/sunday/how-to-get-your-mind-to-read.html

Online Resources

billsullivan, "Exploring a Quandary: Kids Love Nonfiction, But Adults Assume They Don't" PLOS https://scicomm.plos.org/2022/04/27/exploring-a-quandary-kids-love-nonfiction-but-adults-assume-they-dont/

Dr. Sam Bommarito, "About Literacy Instruction - A Letter to the New York Times" doctorsam7 https://doctorsam7.blog/2023/06/12/about-literacy-instruction-a-letter-to-the-new-york-times-by-dr-sam-bommarito/

Building Thinking Classrooms. 14 Practices https://buildingthinkingclassrooms.com/14-practices/#:~:text=A%20thinking%20classroom%20looks%20very,as%20to%20defront%20the%20room.

Nell K. Duke and P. David Pearson, "Effective Practices for Developing Reading Comprehension" Scholastic Red https://faculty.washington.edu/smithant/DukeandPearson.pdf

Joshua Lawrence, "Constrained and unconstrained skill development: Why it matters for secondary students" Readingways https://readingways.org/blog/constrainedand-unconstrained-skill-development

Sarah McClelland, "Scientific Method For Kids With Examples" Little Bins for Little Hands https://littlebinsforlittlehands.com/using-scientific-method-experiments-kids/

National Academy of Education. Reaping the Rewards of Reading for Understanding https://naeducation.org/reaping-the-rewards-of-reading-for-understanding-initiative/

Sarah Schwartz, "Using a Curriculum Rich in Arts, History, and Science Led to Big Reading Improvements" Education Week https://www.edweek.org/teaching-learning/using-a-curriculum-rich-in-arts-history-and-science-led-to-big-reading-improvements/2023/04

Statement from the Knowledge Matters Campaign Scientific Advisory Committee https://knowledgematterscampaign.org/statement-from-the-knowledge-matters-campaign-scientific-advisory-committee/

Melissa Stewart, "5 Kinds of Stem-Themed Nonfiction Books for Kids" PLOS https://scicomm.plos.org/2018/04/10/five-kinds-of-stem-themed-nonfiction-books-for-kids/

Thinking Science https://www.stem.org.uk/system/files/elibrary-resources/2018/11/THINKING%20SCIENCE.pdf

Sharon Vaughn, "The Science of Reading Comprehension: Effective Reading Comprehension Instruction (#2 Spotlight)" https://www.youtube.com/watch?v=s1LHkGXfRdw&t=1s

Natalie Wexler, "More Evidence That Our Approach To Reading Comprehension Is All Wrong" Forbes https://www.forbes.com/sites/nataliewexler/2023/09/04/more-evidence-that-our-approach-to-reading-comprehension-is-all-wrong/?sh=1d73b6846875

Other Books by Adrienne Gear

Reading Power, Revised & Expanded Edition: Teaching students to think while they read (2015)

Nonfiction Reading Power: Teaching students how to think while they read all kinds of information (2008)

Writing Power: Engaging thinking through writing (2011)

Nonfiction Writing Power: Teaching information writing with intent and purpose (2014)

Powerful Understanding: Helping students explore, question, and transform their thinking about themselves and the world around them (2018)

Powerful Writing Structures: Brain pocket strategies for supporting a year-long writing program (2020)

Powerful Poetry: Read, write, rejoice, recite poetry all year (2021)

Index